NOBODY'S GRANDMOTHER

NOBODY'S GRANDMOTHER

STORIES FROM INSIDE AN ELDERLY HOME

GROUP CAPTAIN A C BARUA
(RETD) VSM

Vitasta

Published by
Renu Kaul Verma
Vitasta Publishing Pvt Ltd
2/15, Ansari Road, Daryaganj
New Delhi - 110 002
info@vitastapublishing.com

ISBN: 978-93-90961-83-2

First Edition 2022
MRP ₹495

This collection of stories is entirely a work of fiction. Names, characters, events and incidents are entirely imaginary. Reference to real places, actual regions, institutions or community practices has been made in a fictitious manner. Any resemblance to actual persons, living or dead or actual events is purely coincidental.

Edited by Manjula Lal
Typeset & Cover Design by Somesh Kumar Mishra
Paintings by Col Jiten Hazarika
Printed by Vikas Computer and Printers, New Delhi

CONTENTS

PREFACE

The face has been haunting me for years. Honestly, even today, after 16 years, if I close my eyes, I can vividly see her face mocking me. I failed to help her.

Her skeletal frame, worn-out face with wrinkled skin hanging loose like a cobweb, sunken dark-shadowed eyes, her uncombed knotted hair, her toothless dry lips, her hunched gait, all made me shiver in disbelief and pain. She was completely famished and lost in her ramshackle bamboo shack, surrounded by waist-deep water. A thirty-plus man was lying on a bamboo bed, stiff and groaning with pain.

I had gone to her village, which was around 60 km from Guwahati on a country boat to render humble help to villagers ravaged by a devastating flood in 2005. Her son, a daily wager was the one lying on the bed. He was paralysed because of an untreated back injury sustained due to a fall from a tree he was pruning in the courtyard of his day's employer. Her only source of livelihood came from her part-time job as domestic help, but this too was impossible at that time because of the devastating floods that had ravaged the village. The other inhabitants had already abandoned the area and sought refuge on higher ground. She had stayed back because of her crippled son.

In their scramble for safety, no one had the time to stop to help them. Neither had any relief reached them. The mother-son duo had eaten no food for days and was forced to drink the floodwaters to quench their thirst. The ramshackled one-room bamboo hut still stood there miraculously because of a number of external bamboo props that had supported it. Apart from a few old soot-blackened utensils, a bed with a soiled patchwork quilt, a torn mosquito net and a few dirty clothes hanging from hooks around the hut, it was absolutely empty. I will never forget her face or the scene I saw that day. I was already familiar with poverty and had experienced hunger from very close quarters, but I had never imagined that anyone could be so poor.

Something snapped inside me at that moment. I decided to do something in my own humble way to help such unfortunate people. I returned to Delhi, my home ground, jumped headlong into my various business ventures with the single-minded purpose of earning more money and once I knew I had earned enough, I shut shop, and, left for Guwahati to establish Seneh, a Home for Destitute Old Women, in a plot of land that I owned. This was in 2011. Thanks to people's sympathetic and compassionate gestures and the participation and untiring efforts of a few senior citizens and a bunch of young, dedicated volunteers and caregivers, Seneh today is much-lauded for its service to humanity, especially to destitute old women, and to a lesser extent, to the poor, adolescent girl children studying in rural schools. The destitute are provided shelter, food, clothing and medical care, all free, so that, at least in their sunset years, they can live a life of dignity, comfort and companionship.

A sizeable number of the adolescent girls studying in distant, rural schools, get free menstrual hygiene products every month and a few meritorious girl students receive annual scholarships from the Seneh Trust Fund.

Coming back to the face that has been haunting me, I did return after six years to offer her help, but I could not locate her. Perhaps, my memory of her location in that water-filled expanse had been wrong. My enquiries about the mother-son duo in that area did not bear fruit either.

Through this book, I acknowledge that the memory of that forlorn face is what changed the course of my life; I started experiencing an incredible amount of satisfaction and bliss. It has given me a new understanding of our society and meaning to my life. Once the reader goes through this book, I am sure they will start understanding what I mean.

I know what we are doing is just a dot on the tip of the proverbial iceberg. There is a need for so much more to be done to alleviate the sufferings of the oppressed, the exploited and those unfortunate souls who are pushed around by life's hardships. A small step like ours is an insignificant, minuscule drop in the ocean. But, as they say, little drops combine to make the mighty ocean. Every drop counts.

I dedicate this book to the old residents of Seneh. Each moment that I spend with them can be counted as an invaluable treasure of my life. I feel so happy and content when I am serving them. I especially thank the residents who have allowed me the luxury knowingly, some even without understanding what I am trying to do, to pen their short life stories laced with my own perceptions and imagination. Lapses in the sketches of their lives, if any exist, are completely because of my shortcomings in interpreting their situations and experiences. I am prepared to be guillotined for these shortcomings.

INTRODUCTION

The rocks are huge and black, clinging together like siblings, each dependent on the other for support. They rise high above the ground and have trees sprouting clandestinely up from the gaps between the stones. The early morning rays shine on the weather-beaten faces of the monoliths and the gentle breeze moves the leaves in the trees to a synchronising jig, creating a picturesque setting.

The sturdy structure overlooking this landscape is long, constructed like an 'L', with a very wide veranda. As the rocks glitter in the early morning sun and the birds perched on the trees chirp, the homestead buzzes with activity. The ever-smiling kind nurses Nilima and Janmoni go from room to room, coaxing all the inhabitants to wake up. The no-nonsense chief caretaker Jutika, her gait and demeanour showing who is in charge, is busy bringing in orderliness and decorum. It is a big challenge for the trio, since prayer time, which is almost sacrosanct, is fast approaching.

Their job is tougher than that of most caregivers because the inhabitants are elderly women, all above fifty, some older than eighty. Their aching bodies are reluctant to leave the comfort of their beds, but their spirit always eggs them on. Two of the elderly women have dementia and the eldest inhabitant is the most infirm; all three require gentle prodding and assistance even to go to the toilet. Nilima and Janmoni, the two in-house nurses, bestow them special attention.

There are a number of morning chores to be completed. The residents make their beds, sweep and swab the floors, clean the toilets and complete their morning ablutions. Jutika, the chief caretaker and Trustee, has set very high standards of cleanliness for the house. She is uncompromising in matters of housekeeping. There is a mad rush for the toilets and baths, everyone claiming emergency. Each one is trying to out-manoeuvre the other. She is also busy enforcing discipline.

The cacophony of women tapping on doors and yelling at each other continues for an hour or so till the pandemonium subsides and peace and harmony return. All assemble for the morning prayers, clad in clean clothes, their hair still wet but neatly combed. Absolute calm prevails for the next thirty minutes when the neighbourhood wakes up to the melodious but sober hymns sung in harmony by all the residents belonging to different religions—Hindus, Christians, Muslims and others. All sing together prayers of each religion.

After the prayers, two of the able-bodied boarders, detailed by turn, cook breakfast for all. Those chosen are required to cook all meals for the day according to fixed timings. Two others, who are not cooks, but are good at chopping the vegetables and washing the utensils, assist them. Once breakfast is announced, they all file in, the visually impaired and physically challenged being helped in by others. Each one occupies her permanently allotted seat. Breakfast passes off peacefully, occasional whines and complaints notwithstanding.

Post breakfast, they are all required to linger a little longer in their seats. Enters Janmoni, the ever-smiling and ebullient young nurse a medicine tray in hand. She checks, rechecks and thereafter, hands over medicines to almost all for the different ailments they suffer from.

The ailments vary from diabetes, hypertension, thyroiditis and others, all mostly psychosomatic. The nurse's task is not easy, as she has to keep a close watch on Jinu, who stubbornly refuses to believe that she requires the psychiatric drugs prescribed for her and protests vigorously. No amount of persuasion will convince Jinu, the suave graduate with a history of frequent depression, to take the psychiatric tablets. Jutika has found a way to administer the drugs to the reluctant ones: the tablets are powdered and mixed with the curry. Initially, the patient complains about bitterness in the curry, but gradually, they get used to it. Again, there is Manju, who stealthily keeps the drug concealed under her tongue to spit it out at an opportune moment. However, Janmoni ensures she swallows it in her presence.

As the day progresses, most of the twenty-five-odd elderly women residing in the house are engrossed in their creative tasks. The immensely talented Gita is busy with her sewing machine to stitch dresses or with her embroidery. Occasionally, she walks to the handloom corner to advise Niru and Mohini, who are concentrating on their work, busy weaving magic. At times, Jinu goes to the loom to help and to learn, but Mohini's words offend her, and she starts sobbing like a baby until Jutika steps in to restore peace.

Sarala, who is visually impaired, picks up her harmonium and practises her musical skills. Vivian and Arti are occupied in making delicate foot mats from old torn saris or jute ropes; Shefali, Sadhana, and Sukhi are playing Ludo. Devi and Milu, the oldest among the residents, are sitting idly on the bench kept on the veranda, seemingly oblivious of the activities around them. The dementia-afflicted Lazbonti is yelling at them to lift their legs, because she is re-swabbing the veranda, while Purnima, Kusum and Tulu are in the kitchen, chopping vegetables for lunch.

Ashalata, the laziest of them all, is trying to doze off and Nilima with her typical commanding loud voice is yelling at her. Anamika, the one who is hearing and speech impaired, is shrieking at Kunjalata, the differently-abled, for some flimsy reason. Priyabala, unnoticed by anyone, is quietly lying on her bed, dozing off. Bina is pacing up and down the verandah muttering unintelligible words. Suddenly, there is a loud shout of alarm from the otherwise quiet and withdrawn Swapna, a depression patient, who is busy collecting night jasmine flowers fallen from the tree that stands majestically in the courtyard.

Suddenly Swapna shrieks in alarm on seeing Rahima, the mentally unstable, differently-abled harmless new member trying to scale the locked iron gate to venture out. Jutika who is by now busy with office work rushes out and intercepts Rahima to prevent her from escaping. Rahima is under treatment but is yet to stabilise.

Sukhi is making footmats from jute thread. Manju is trying to write one more poem, which she will hand over to me the following day for corrections. Amma is muttering loudly in Tamil, the only language she knows, but no one understands what she is trying to convey. She talks to herself without bothering to know what is happening around her. Faguni is staring vacantly at nobody, busy with her own thoughts, which the psychiatrist is yet to decipher.

All that I have described above is a typical day at the house for destitute old women in their sunset years, all so dramatic and so very true. The house overlooking the mountain of rocks is named 'Seneh', meaning eternal love in Assamese. The residents were from different nooks and corners, with diverse backgrounds. They all have suffered humiliation, neglect and cruelty, but are now bound by a common thread of love and compassion. Fate played havoc in their pasts, making them so vulnerable that, but for the intervention of the people who run the house, quite a few of them would have perished, unwept and unsung.

Each one of them has a touching story to tell. The common features in their stories portray the ugly face of humanity, human bondage and sufferings, life's triumphs and tribulations, emotions and ego, apathy and neglect, and most strikingly, their indomitable struggle to live on crumbs. We at the house feel blessed to have intervened and rehabilitated them with loving kindness and care.

In the succeeding chapters, I will describe how they survived through the misery and cruelty that fate and the world imposed on them. Some of them shared with me about their pasts, with truthfulness, without hesitance. which I have incorporated them generously in the stories of their lives. Given their mental and physical state, some stories have numerous gaps. I have filled these gaps with my perception and imagination and to that extent, some of their stories are partly fictionalised.

Actually, six of the residents do not even know where they hail from or their real names. Most of them were picked up from the streets in mentally unstable conditions. In their case, their pasts, as narrated by me are figments of my own imagination, interspersed with bits of unverifiable information, and my perception about how they became prey to the evils of society and to the utter callousness of people who call themselves human.

Out of the lot of forty women, including the departed, and a few reunited with their families, I have selected only twenty to write about because of different reasons. A few were reluctant to allow me to write about them. And as mentioned earlier, a few others had hardly any memory about their past for me to establish any leads to piece together their lives. As for the rest that I have not written about—honestly, I did not find their past lives interesting, although they did not object to being written about.

What is gratifying and heartening, however, is that today, they are a very happy lot, have a unique family life, and I am sure, if the reader decides to visit them at 31, Nizara Path, Narakasur, Kahilipara, Guwahati, Assam, India, they will be delighted to discover the truth of the smiles in their faces today.

While narrating the saga of their lives, I have tried to give the reader a fair glimpse of Assamese rural society: how they live with nature, the rural surroundings, their beliefs and dogmas, how they solemnise festivities. Some of the practices may look weird to an urban reader, but they give a kaleidoscopic view of a vibrant, happy, peace-loving, content society that, till recently, lived in perfect harmony with nature, accepting its bounties and furies with philosophical and dignified solemnity. Acts of God are not meant for humans to challenge. Unfortunately, materialistic pursuits and the lure from external influences are gradually eroding this bonhomie with nature, with the result that peace and tranquillity are taking a beating.

ACKNOWLEDGEMENTS

I wish to thank my wife Dipali, daughter Rashmi, son Amar and daughter-in-law Priya for their encouragement. I also acknowledge my gratitude to Jutika for her unflinching loyalty to the cause and for her invaluable help in piecing together the lives of those whose bio-sketches make up this book.

No words can express my gratitude to Col Jiten Hazarika, the well-known painter who allowed me to use his paintings in the book and on the cover page. I express my gratitude to Reena Singh, journalist, and her writer, scholar, journalist husband, Oswald Pereira, who did the editing of the manuscript.

I thank my friend Mrs Mitra Phukan, the much acclaimed writer and columnist, for her encouragement and guidance.

I also thank the young, energetic writer Madhulika Liddle who helped me and encouraged me from the beginning to write this book and my learned friends Dr Udayan Mishra and his worthy wife,

Dr Tilotttama Mishra (both prolific writers) for their back-thumping and no-holds-barred criticisms after I gave them the manuscript to read and comment.

Priyabala Karmakar

The First Resident

She was fascinated by the azure sky that was dotted with specks of grey, like driftwood floating down a river. The clouds wore caps of white fur, like old Eskimos. They moved slowly, as if tired of carrying loads of moisture for long periods. From the gentle, cool breeze blowing into her nostrils, carrying the sweet, soothing fragrance of the blooming xewali (night jasmine) flowers, Priyabala knew that the enchanting months of autumn had arrived. She loved autumn.

She loved to walk barefoot on the wet grass with diamond-like dewdrops hanging from the blades, offering a vista of hope and serenity after months of being battered by torrential rains accompanied by noisy storms. The area is prone to nature's fury because of its location in one of the wettest places on earth.

Priyabala looked up to the banyan tree under which she sat pondering upon her next step. She admired the jovial mood of the not-so-young leaves that danced merrily, swaying in the gentle breeze. Wasn't she just like these leaves, she mused? From the day they were born, the leaves had been withstanding the pressure of life's realities, fighting for survival. A few of the leaves, probably the weaker ones that were devoid of confidence had long perished, drifting away to be trampled and eventually decay, lost for eternity. Others would fight doggedly on, and survive the worst of squalls. They were the ones which were dancing in merriment now, the rhythm of the gentle breeze of autumn giving poise and grace to their dance.

'Why can't I be like them?' wondered Priyabala. From the day the leaves were born, they had been fighting against their existential vulnerability, and had been standing firm in their resolve to conquer challenges. 'Is it not true that all of God's creations are ordained to jump, knowingly or unknowingly, into the unknown, even if it appears dark and uncertain, the only instinct egging it on being the spirit of hope—the hope that at the end of the tunnel, light will appear in all probability? So why should she be static?'

The decision made, she walked back to their house

and stood in front of the old mirror that was dotted with black spots, like a fallen green leaf in the early process of decay. What she saw pleased her. The brownish skin was taut and smooth, free of scars or pimples. The high cheekbones gave prominence to her long pointed nose, more so because of the flat contours of her forehead. When she smiled, the muscles near her lips contracted, making a tiny dimple at either end. The broad unplucked eyebrows gave an aura of geniality to her large bright eyes. Her black hair was parted and tied neatly with red ribbons into two long braids.

She looked like a fairy princess, trying to place her feet on an unknown tract of land. Understandably, she was apprehensive but determined, emboldened by the decision taken under the banyan tree.

Unlike the path taken by the Buddha that paved the way to his salvation, she was to plunge headlong into the unknown, without giving a thought to the consequences. She would stealthily ride the night bus with the little money she had and land up at Guwahati the next morning, whence she would try to write a new chapter of her life.

She was an immensely confident girl of eighteen, her robust health and inward courage her wealth; her motivation was her capacity to work hard without looking for comfort or appreciation, or succumbing to false notions of dignity.

Priyabala was born into a Hira potter's family in a remote village near North Lakhimpur, a small town on the north bank of the Brahmaputra in Assam. The Hiras bore the title of Karmakar. Karmakars are traditional potters who usually settled in areas where the particularly sticky clay they used for their pottery was found in abundance. The clay was ideal for moulding into different shapes. The village had twelve such families living in Hira Para, meaning the hamlet of the Hiras.

Priyabala's father was an irresponsible and impetuous man for whom pursuing pleasure mattered more than work. He would much rather spend his time fishing with his tackle than lend a helping hand to his wife in making earthen pots and utensils. Pottery was traditionally a woman's vocation, with the men helping to collect the clay in February-March, along with the white sand required for the process. The clay was stored in a trench dug into the earth and pounded with a wooden stick. Traditionally, the men also helped in lighting the hearth. Priyabala's father, however, had no time to render this help, other than collecting the clay–a task which he performed very grudgingly.

He had four children, Priyabala being the eldest. When Priya was eleven years old, her mother passed away after a brief illness, leaving the children in the care of her husband. He, however, had no time for them. To add to their misery, they were extremely poor. The entire responsibility of looking after her younger siblings, as well as making the pots fell on Priyabala's tender shoulders. But two of her siblings, a boy of two years and a girl of five, died in quick succession because of malnutrition and lack of care.

Neighbours and relatives did come to help but they themselves were fighting hard to make both ends meet, since the demand for pottery was gradually being eroded by plastic products. One day, when Priyabala was fifteen, her father rowed out on the river in a country boat made of driftwood to catch fish with a friend. He never returned. After five days, the bloated bodies of the two friends were recovered 8-km downstream.

Their uncle took the two orphans to his home and took on the entire responsibility of bringing them up. He was a kind and benevolent man who did not distinguish between his own children and the brother-sister duo.

This was not true of his wife, who grudged their presence and would often display her wrath and scold them on the slightest pretext. 'But in all fairness, I must admit that she never denied us food and showed concern and compassion when my brother fell ill. She even scolded me because I neglected him once,' says Priyabala, now a septuagenarian.

'Even today, I remember the bus ride to Gauhati (now Guwahati). Since I paid less, I was allotted the last row. It was a very rough ride. The gravel-topped road had huge potholes after the fury of the rains. While negotiating these potholes, the rear end of the bus was really bumpy, throwing us up and then smashing us down on to the wooden bench on which we were sitting. My bones creaked and back pained for days,' Priyabala narrates.

On the bus, she had met a man from her village. He asked her what she planned to do at Guwahati. She said she did not know. 'The only thing I know is I want change and freedom. Above all, it is my belief that I have a strong will and an equally strong body. That will see me through,' she had said.

The man took her to his home, a two-room thatched cottage in the foothills of the Nilachal hills. His wife and three children welcomed her. He was a salesman in a hardware shop and lived on a pittance. Occasionally, the wife would work at a construction site as a helper to a mason and earn small sums to augment their resources. Priyabala started accompanying her and working as a labourer. There she befriended a middle-aged woman. Through her, she got a job as a nanny to look after the newborn child of a famous Assamese folk musician couple. (This son is the renowned singer and composer Papan Mahanta, famous all over India).

Priyabala says, 'They were an extremely considerate and compassionate couple. Papan was the apple of my eye. But my brother, who joined me at Guwahati later, spoiled the broth. He created some misunderstandings which forced me to leave them.' (I have taken her statement at face value and never felt the need to check it, although I know the family.)

Priyabala left her job as a nanny unannounced and once again started working as a labourer at a construction site. There, she met a young mason who started wooing her. After a six-month courtship, they were married and started living in a small rented house. Their conjugal life was smooth except that they could not conceive a child. Life was tough, work was not always forthcoming and when they did find work, the remuneration did not match the hard work they both put in. But getting two square meals a day was never an issue till her husband began drinking. Prior to that, they had no marital discord.

Twice, they migrated from Guwahati looking for work. For a year or so, they lived in Tezpur, the beautiful town on the north bank of the mighty Brahmaputra. Once, they lived in Sibsagar for a year, another beautiful historical town.

She is unsure about what made him a drunkard. Was it the fact that they could not have a child? But knowing Priyabala, it could have also been her demanding and nagging nature. She was adept at making an issue out of a non-issue. But this is true for the majority of poor households in India, so let us not hazard a guess about why he turned alcoholic. The fact was that he turned to drink for solace and all of Priyabala's efforts to wean him away from alcohol proved futile.

Nevertheless, they lived together for a good thirty years, and managed to buy a small plot of land on top of a hill with a mud pathway, where they constructed a small cottage with bamboo walls and a tin roof. For two years, their life fell into a predictable pattern. The man would go for work, come back late completely sozzled on country liquor, invariably pick a fight with Priyabala, go to bed after eating a light meal and snore like a dragon.

She would shed tears, blaming fate for her plight, while looking at her sleeping husband with pity and love. Finally, she would succumb to a restless sleep full of nightmares. At times, she would go and find work for herself, buy a few items of clothing with the money she earned, and ensure that next morning when sober, her otherwise loving husband dressed up neatly, had a heavy breakfast of rice, *dal* and roasted potato along with a green chilli that he loved.

She would also pack a small lunch and hand it over to him in an aluminium box, then see him off. Finally, she would start her household chores that included fetching water from the well around a hundred metres down the hill and washing the clothes on the bank of the well itself. She would then set off to collect firewood from the nearby jungle. It was customary for her to visit her neighbours in the afternoon hours, indulge in gossip with the other women and invariably have her afternoon tea in the house of the Hazarikas, who were very close to her.

She voluntarily helped the lady of the house in domestic chores, mainly attending to the demands of her children, specially the youngest, a little boy. She lamented her own lack of a child and cried secretly, wondering why God did not consider her worthy to beget a child. But she never betrayed her sorrow to others. Mrs Hazarika could probably feel the void in Priyabala's heart, and hence the good lady allowed her to look after the youngest son and enjoy his childish pranks. Unlike most possessive mothers, she never grudged the chemistry that developed between the child and Priyabala. On the other hand, she encouraged it. Thus, at fifty-eight, Priyabala's life finally took on a definite pattern, her morning hours busy with her own routine, her afternoons spent in socialising and in artificially trying to fill the void in her heart, and her evenings in hoping against all hope that her husband would come back early, sober and not staggering.

She was completely at ease with her life, neither complaining nor whining till fate delivered a heavy blow and her life then took an ugly turn.

It was winter. A light drizzle accompanied by a gentle breeze and an overcast sky brought the day to an end earlier than usual. Priyabala was sitting alone at home, a light fire of twigs warming her body, when suddenly, she heard footsteps coming up the hill towards her house. She came out to find a few of her husband's colleagues walking towards her. She searched for her husband's face among them. That is when she noticed that they looked crestfallen.

She instantly knew something terrible had happened. Before she could utter a word, one of the visitors told her to come with them. Her husband, they said, was lying sprawled on the roadside, motionless, his body as cold as ice, unresponsive. She ran in utter panic, the others following.

Her pace became faster. At the curb, she found a crowd around a body. She stopped, gasping for breath, then hurled herself on the lifeless body of her husband. He was long dead. She wailed. Someone from the crowd lifted her up, away from the lifeless body; a woman from a nearby house took care of her and tried to console her. By around eight in the night, word of his demise had also reached their neighbours. Hazarika and his wife came, and took control of the situation, organised his funeral. By the time the body was cremated and the last rites completed, the sun appeared above the horizon. Priyabala came home, lonely, crestfallen and completely devastated.

It took her ten days to recover from the shock and trauma. The neighbours, especially the Hazarikas, were extremely helpful and caring. They would give her company by turn, provide her meals, and try to cheer her up. The nights were, however, extremely lonely and frightening. She would be awake, unable to comprehend a life without her husband and would doze off till nightmares woke her up. In ten days, she looked older by ten years. But at the end, the resolute and strong-willed Priyabala resurfaced. She decided to go to work, keep busy and earn her livelihood without fear. Life must go on, she resolved.

The construction company where her husband worked gave her a lighter but engrossing job. The co-workers were considerate, the supervisor lenient. Soon she fell into a routine. Every morning at eight, she would take her tiffin box and walk the 1.5 km to her workplace, work till four in the evening, then walk back home humming a tune, cook her meal and retire early. Whenever she felt lonely and missed her husband, she would play her small transistor radio at full volume and try to hum along with the songs being played. She also started saving money to buy a television.

On her way back from work, she had made it a habit to visit the Hazarikas, play a while with the young one, drink a cup of tea and climb back, tired, to her hamlet. She had resigned herself to her fate, and as she said, she 'discovered a strange happiness in loneliness'.

But alas! God was unwilling to spare her this happiness also. Another nasty and cruel blow to her life came suddenly, throwing her completely off-balance for life. While on her way home from work, one summer evening, a speeding car smashed into her. Both her hands and a leg were crushed under the weight of the tyres. Her hip, too, was fractured.

Some passers-by came running, and hailing a passing car, they took her to the nearest hospital. A person had also noted down the number of the car that hit her. It was a hit-and-run case. She was in hospital for more than three months. When she was discharged, her right hand was almost paralysed, the hand scarred with marks of damaged skin and muscle, the implanted iron piece in her hip making movement not only extremely difficult, but also very painful.

Even with the support of a heavy stick, she could not walk more than a few laboured steps. Without help, she could not climb the hill to reach her hamlet. The neighbours once again came forward to help and somehow managed her affairs. The Hazarikas ensured a square meal at her bedside, every day without fail.

In the meantime, the police succeeded in nabbing the errant driver who turned out to be a middle-aged businessman. His car was impounded and he was charged with negligent driving. He was arraigned in a court of law. Her well-wishers arranged a competent lawyer to represent her and he managed to produce six eyewitnesses in her favour. The accused knew he would be fighting a watertight case against him and opted for an out-of-court settlement.

Priyabala's lawyer readily agreed. According to the settlement, the accused would pay a compensation of Rs 1.5 lakh. In addition, he would also foot the entire hospital bill.

It was quite a decent sum, so there was jubilation till the lawyer announced that out of the compensation amount he collected on Priyabala's behalf, he would retain one-third as his fee, and another one-third had been committed as payment to the witnesses. Hence her share would be only Rs 50,000. The neighbours protested and threatened the lawyer, but it was of no use. A crippled Priyabala had to be content with the Rs 50,000 to sustain her for the rest of her life.

Out of this amount, she had to repay an amount of Rs 23,000 to a few neighbours from whom she had borrowed money in the interim. So, in effect, she was left with only Rs 27,000. This amount saw her through for the next six months. At the end of this period, she had no financial support, nor was she physically capable of earning her livelihood. As a last resort, she sold off her plot of land for a paltry Rs 12,000 with the provision that she could remain in the house for as long as she desired. Actually, the land was an encroachment on government land with no legal papers, hence the paltry sum.

'Seneh' was established in June 2011, with the aim to bring succour to destitute old women by providing them a home with all amenities free to live a life of comfort and dignity. Unfortunately, for two months, no one was willing to come and stay. One lady did come with an understanding that her small pet pariah dog would also be accommodated. We readily agreed. But her demand for a small secluded area in the room that had been designed to accommodate four, for establishing an idol of a goddess, could not be conceded. The rules specified that no individual religious activity of any particular faith would be allowed within the precincts. The adamant lady chose to go back to living under a bridge, braving the vagaries of nature.

We came to know about Priyabala through word of mouth. We decided to go and meet her at her residence just after sunrise. It was a winter month, although the winter is never very harsh in this part of the country.

From a distance, Mr Hazarika pointed her out to us—an old and extremely frail lady laboriously trying to negotiate a climb with all her might, supporting her weight on a bamboo stick in her left hand. Her right hand was in a sling. Her loose, unkempt hair was hanging like the roots of a recently uprooted fern. Her tattered clothes hung loose on her bent body. Every few minutes, she would rest a while, gather her strength, adjust her shawl and take a long breath before contemplating the next step.

It was a pathetic sight of human suffering and yet there was the inherent spirit to fight on against insurmountable odds.

Accompanied by Mrs Hazarika, we accosted her and reasoned with her to abandon her cottage and shift to Seneh. We promised that we would take good care of her and she would have no reasons to complain. Perhaps she did not believe us or was it normal human behaviour to resist plunging into the unknown, preferring to keep hanging onto the only support, even if it was a mere straw?

Priyabala refused point-blank to leave her dilapidated abode. No amount of pleading, cajoling, or arguing could convince her. She remained adamant. We left disappointed. The next morning, we got a call from Mr Hazarika: they had somehow convinced her to pay a visit to our establishment and see Seneh with her own eyes to decide if we were trustworthy. They came, she was pleased with what she saw, but remained apprehensive.

It was decided that she would stay at Seneh for a couple of days to help her make up her mind. Next morning, we got her in without her belongings, as she refused to shift lock, stock and barrel. Our sincerity, the care provided by Nilima who was the only nurse initially and the serene atmosphere convinced her she was, indeed, in safe hands. She never went back even to fetch her personal belongings.

Thus, Priyabala became the first resident and beneficiary of our humble efforts. Almost instantly, a mother-daughter relationship bloomed between

Priyabala and Nilima. Needless to say, I also developed a special relationship with her, a relationship based on her trust in me, and her complete faith that I could do nothing that was contrary to her interests. Her faith and concern for me always gives me strength.

It required a lot of effort, the help of a trained physiotherapist whom we temporarily hired, regular massages thrice a day, and innumerable visits to the orthopaedics department at Guwahati Medical College, before Priyabala was able to move around unsupported and even help Nilima and the others in household jobs. It took almost six months for Priyabala to become completely independent.

For the first three months, Nilima worked relentlessly as if she was her shadow, helping her to move around, bathe her, help her dress, comb her hair, feed her, and nurse her wounds, give her massages and medication. After she was up and about, her eyes were operated upon for cataract. Later, it was Priyabala who would welcome new residents, help them settle in, and advise them about the dos and don'ts.

She soon started behaving like an elderly matron, much to the chagrin of the others. They visibly resented her interference and big sister attitude. Quite often, it was left to us to intervene and settle disputes, since she would not pay heed to Nilima's diktats.

But hidden behind her brazen and somewhat rude

exterior, there was a kind and soft woman. If someone was sick, she is invariably the first to nurse and help her and pester us to call the doctor. She has developed an emotional relationship with Dr Kalpana Saikia, Seneh's volunteer lady doctor, who provided yeomen service to the residents of Seneh till ill health came in her way. Their binding relationship far exceeded a doctor-patient one.

Days passed by. Life at Seneh moved on. After a poor start, Seneh began to attract a lot of appreciation and people's support. The beds were soon filled to capacity. In fact, it had to be doubled in about two years because of increase in the demand. Welfare and entertainment activities have mushroomed with the participation of the supportive public. Priyabala became an enthusiastic participant in all these activities that included group singing and dancing and development of hobbies.

There were, and still are, verbal duels, squabbles, a little shedding of tears here and there, and occasional sulking as is wont to happen in a family with thirty-odd old sisters living under the same roof with a couple of girls, less than half their ages being called upon to control and administer them. Priyabala like everyone else, has been very much a part of these episodes.

Again, fate dealt a blow. She had a mild fever accompanied by cough which persisted in spite of prolonged medications including antibiotics. When nothing helped, she was sent to the Guwahati Medical

College for further diagnosis. To our horror, she was diagnosed with an advanced stage of tuberculosis.

She was admitted to the hospital and remained there for a couple of months. Our two nurses, turn by turn, attended to her round the clock. About a week into her hospitalisation, she began to display strange behaviour, as if, she had become mentally unsound. She became abusive, abrasive and aggressive.

But the doctors attending to her opined that it was a normal reaction to the medication she was being administered, and that these side-effects would disappear within a week. They did.

She returned after a month's hospitalisation. Lest the disease spread, we carved out a secluded area to quarantine her. A high-protein diet, regular medication and nursing played the trick. She remained in quarantine for almost three months, till a blood and sputum examination declared her cured. Medication, however, continued for another two months. Thereafter her ordeal ended. She was allowed to emerge from quarantine. Priyabala became her old self again.

If you visit Seneh, the beaming Priyabala, an embodiment of struggle and courage, who fought and overcame the tribulations of life, will certainly be there to greet you with her signature broad, coy smile hanging on her lips.

Devi Bhujang

A Saga Of Loss And Rehabilitation

The pathway to the small brook was narrow. The overnight rain had made it slippery. The wild foliage on both sides was thick and lush green. The puddles that had formed because of the rains made the path difficult, needing to be negotiated with caution and care. If she took even a single careless step, it would result in a nasty fall and spilling of the water she was carrying from the brook in two Dalda (hydrogenated vegetable oil) cans. Holes were pierced on opposite sides of the cans to tie the jute rope for ease of carrying the cans.

Occasionally, Devi would put down her water-filled cans, pluck a wild flower, smell it, and tuck it into her neatly combed hair, replacing the one she had put earlier.

She would also go deep inside the foliage to pluck and eat a few wild berries. Throughout her uphill journey, she would check whether the white stone was still tucked into the waist of her knee-length pyjama. For the last one month or so, she had been collecting one white stone every day from the rivulet's bed. Today's treasure was special, since it was shaped like a small elephant.

The nine-year-old was named Devi since she was born on the day of Mahastami, which is considered the most auspicious and sacred of the five-day long Durga Puja festival. The goddess is called by scores of names, Devi being one of them.

Devi was a beautiful girl. Her eyes were light blue with flowing eyebrows. (Alas! How could someone inflict such injuries on one of those eyes? We will discuss that later).

Every morning, her mother would comb her long hair, and part it neatly into two braids, which she tied with the faded red ribbon that her father had bought for her from the weekly Sunday market. Her father used to regularly trek the 12 km to the market to barter his produce for essentials. She was probably the loveliest young girl in the village as the villagers used to call her 'Little Beauty'.

Devi's family lived in the hamlet atop a hillock located in a remote area of Nepal. There were forty-three houses in the village. Behind the hillock stood the majestic mountain range. The slopes on the four sides were full of corn fields. Across the rivulet, there were large paddy fields owned by three or four wealthy families of the village, all with the family name, Rana, the rich warrior class of Nepal.

In addition to sowing his own corn fields, Devi's father cultivated paddy on a plot of land that a landowner had leased to him. Out of the crop, as per their agreement, he retained one-third, and the remainder went to the landlord. In his own field, he cultivated mustard after the corn was harvested. He also grew seasonal vegetables in the small plot of undulating land behind their house.

Devi's father was probably the strongest man in the village, his muscular body the envy of every young man in the area. He was a specialist in the use of the *khukri* (small sword) and was always in demand for severing the heads of goats in one stroke that were sacrificed to please the goddess. They were a very happy family, the five of them, that included three children. They would always wait for the *puja* festivities, which would bring a generous portion of the goat meat sacrificed for the deity. Her mother would make a very spicy preparation of the meat. Their eyes would water because of the hot spices, but they relished it.

As she laboriously approached her house, she could clearly hear the sound of her father's coughing. From his hoarse long cough, she knew her father would spit out streaks of blood. In the last six months, her father's muscular body had turned into a skeleton because of the incurable sickness that occurs when the ugly witch touches the body on very cold, dark and wet nights!

The village sorcerer had been trying different methods to drive away the evil spirit that had taken refuge in her father's body but to no avail. For his well-being, her mother had vowed she would offer a buffalo for sacrifice on the altar of the goddess next autumn. Devi was hopeful that once that was done, her father would be able to walk steadily again, work in the fields and bring her a new ribbon and probably a nice clip for her hair. But the autumn *puja* was still a month away. Would he be able to weather the storm till then?

One night, she suddenly woke up hearing her mother sobbing. In a very feeble voice, her father was telling her mother, 'I do not know how you are going to survive. I am extremely worried about the children, especially Devi. She is so beautiful, endearing and kind-hearted.' He took a laboured breath and continued, 'I know my life is ending. I assure you that wherever my soul resides after my death, I will always keep an eye on you all. Please be brave. Have faith in the goddess. She will guide you.'

Her mother tried to assure him that he had more of a life to live. 'The autumn festival is a few days away. I have already arranged a young buffalo for the sacrifice. Once done, the goddess will bless us, and you will be up again,' she said. Devi's father sighed heavily but did not utter a word.

Next morning, he passed away. And Devi's life changed forever.

***

In due course, Devi turned fifteen. After her father's death, they lived a very hard life for a year till a widower, tall and lean, started coming to their house, helping her mother in the fields and also supporting the family financially. Initially, Devi accepted him, although she noticed his weakness for her mother, until he started living in the house. Devi could never fathom the idea of him replacing her father and sleeping on the bed her father had used.

One fine day, she walked out of the house with her younger brother and took refuge in her uncle's house. The uncle was very kind and loving. It was his wife whom they loathed and despised. She always considered them a burden and made Devi and her young brother toil hard, day in and day out. Devi was required to do the household work and also look after the cattle and milk the cows every morning and evening.

Tez Bahadur Bhujong was a domestic hand who helped her uncle in the fields and also collected fodder for the cattle. He lived in an outhouse. In addition to free food, he earned a paltry sum as his wage, which was not commensurate with the amount of work he put in. He was, however, not one to complain. He was a milksop, a minion. But he was kind and full of compassion. And what attracted her to him were his broad shoulders, muscular body, like her father's, and a very soft and endearing voice. Above all, his ability to work hard and also to weave magic with bamboo and cane, clinched her attraction for him. The icing on the cake was the way he played the flute before he went to sleep. It would stir her mind, body and soul.

He too thought of Devi as his sweetheart – slim, lithe and beautiful her sidelong love-lorn glances penetrating his heart like lightning.

He was at her disposal, ready to sacrifice all his comforts for her sake and plunge into the unknown. Ultimately, they did exactly that. One dark night, with whatever little money he had, they eloped. They trekked down the hills, taking the most hazardous route because of the lurking fear that they would be hunted out. Even the whisper of the leaves would startle them. They clung to each other, like twins in a mother's womb, connected by the same umbilical cord; he occasionally helped her when negotiating the rapids cascading down the hills like she was a rosebud beginning to open its petals loaded with fragrance and beauty.

After three days of arduous trekking, they reached a hamlet of around thirty houses near the Nepal-India border. Here lived one of Tez Bahadur's distant cousins who worked in the fields of a Madhesi landlord. He gave them shelter and food. After a few day's rest, Tez Bahadur also picked up a job of looking after the cattle of the landlord. For his work, he earned a small sum. They cleared a small area in the jungle nearby, constructed a hut of bamboo and wood with a thatched roof and started living there.

It was good living for a year, till one day, they heard a rumour that Devi's uncle had found out about their whereabouts, and two of his cronies were on their way to accost them.

In no time, they bundled up their belongings and fled to the nearby rail head. Devi was five months pregnant. They took a train eastward into India and got down at Bongaigaon. In the train, a country cousin befriended them and took them to his village on the Assam-Bhutan border. This is where they lived thereafter.

Tez Bahadur picked up a job as a farm hand in a house of a local landlord. The landlord gave them shelter. In his spare time, Tez Bahadur started making cane and bamboo household items and sold it to a merchant who visited him once a month. He made a paltry sum which they saved. Devi also started working as a maid in the household. Her first baby was a female child who died when she was just one month because of a 'yellowing' ailment, probably jaundice.

By the time their second child, once again a baby girl, was born, the couple had managed to acquire a small piece of land and had constructed their own house. Within a couple of years, Devi had a son. In the meantime, they had saved enough to purchase a small piece of cultivable land and started their own farm. Demand for Tez's handicrafts also increased.

The fourth child, a girl, came into their life. Both the parents toiled hard; they had two milch cows and a couple of bulls. The flock of poultry and the pariah dog that took refuge in their courtyard complemented each other. Theirs was a typical rural household whose needs were limited to two square meals, bare minimum clothes and a straw bed on which to sleep at night. The couple were so busy catering for these bare necessities that they had no time to dream of educating their children or of making provisions for future uncertainties. And since their needs and aspirations were limited, they lived a life of love and contentment, tied to each other like a bunch of bananas that cannot be separated unless ripped apart.

But fate did rip them apart.

A cloudburst and the resultant deluge was not uncommon in that part of the country. The river flowing gently at a considerable distance from their house would always carry away the excess water, leaving enough in the fields for the paddy crop to be nurtured. It was Nature's gift and they always sent up a prayer of thanks. But this time it was different. The deluge continued unabated for days. The embankment could not withstand the pressure of the overflowing water.

First they heard a distant gurgle. The gurgle escalated into a hoarse rumble. The cows started mooing, the hens croaking and the dog barking. Tez Bahadur went running out, unleashed the cows and then he saw it. It came roaring and thundering, a giant wave of foaming water, inundating everything in its path, destroying houses and cattle sheds and carrying along with it cattle and poultry. A few cattle swam to higher plateaus. Others perished.

Tez ran back, commanded his wife to take the children fast to the nearby plateau and collected whatever he could of their belongings. He swam back in neck-deep water, made a raft out of banana trunks, went to his home, collected a few other items including rice and two of his hens, and rowed back.

He made a second trip with Devi on board to retrieve whatever else they could, but just when they were near it, his thatched house caved in and collapsed. Their dog and an unknown cat were found atop the floating roof, both clinging for their lives, forgetting their genetic rivalry. Tez Bahadur and Devi got both of them aboard. While rowing back to the safety of the height, they saw a small child being washed away. Tez Bahadur jumped into the swelling waters, lifted the child and brought him to the raft.

But it was too late. The child was bloated with swallowed water and although they tried hard to revive her, she died. They came ashore with the lifeless body. By that time, the plateau was crowded with others. Seeing the child, a young mother came forward and when she found her child's lifeless body, she howled and wailed like a baby. Her husband came running and took the mother and the dead child away.

For seven days, they lived on the plateau, surviving on a single meal a day that was distributed by a relief agency. Occasionally, they had rice soaked with flood water since they had no provisions to cook; they slept inside makeshift tents. The children played the whole day with other children, drank the abundant flood water to quench their thirst and caught small fish in the puddles left behind by the receding waters. The scorching sun baked their naked skins, filling every inch with prickly heat that they kept on scratching with one hand while playing with the other.

The elders kept busy gossiping till the receding waters made it possible to wade through the mud and return to what was left of their homes. They then embarked on reconstructing their damaged huts. Devi, assisted by her eldest, got busy collecting driftwood and stored it in their courtyard to be used later as firewood. Before they could settle in, a cholera epidemic broke out, with devastating results.

The first victim in Devi's family was their youngest daughter who succumbed to severe dehydration because of the unabated vomiting and diarrhoea. Before they had time to wipe their tears, their son fell victim to it on the third day. Devi did not cry, wail or pound her chest in grief. Instead, she stared long at the lifeless body of her son as if she had been struck by lightning. Her mind went completely blank.

She kept standing there like a figure of clay, incapable of feeling or moving till her husband shook her to life. They heard news of families getting completely wiped out in days, and people leaving their village in panic. They, too, decided to leave. But that evening, her husband suddenly fell ill with the same symptoms vomiting and loose watery stools. Devi ran helter-skelter for help. But except for a few white tablets, she got nothing. On the fourth day, he also succumbed, leaving Devi with her only surviving daughter. A few neighbours brought her husband's body to the courtyard from their house. Devi kept staring at his lifeless rigid body without batting an eyelid. Someone tried to shake her to life, but to no avail. She stood rigid like a stone. Then suddenly, she started laughing loudly and uncontrollably. And from that moment onwards, her world changed for ever.

The main occurrences narrated above are true, but let me inform my learned readers, the graphic details are figments of my imaginations. I heard about Devi from an old lady whom I chanced upon on a bus ride. She told me about how the residents of her village are torturing an old woman whom they believe is possessed and has brought bad luck to the village.

Next weekend, along with Nilima, the nurse and a driver, I travelled to Kumrikata, the place where I was to meet the lady whom I met earlier on the bus. The road was bumpy and difficult to negotiate. By the time we reached, it was midday. Since Nilima's house was on the way, we stopped by, picked up Nilima's mother and started for the village of the informer. The village is mostly inhabited by Nepalese settlers.

By that time, word had got around in the village about our impending arrival and the purpose of our visit. The villagers were excited. If we took Devi away, the scourge would go away, they thought. They scoured the village looking for her. An elderly school teacher told us that Devi feared the villagers and specially the children who invariably pelted stones at her whenever she appeared. Devi would normally seek refuge in the nearby jungles or in some secluded corner till the pangs of hunger forced her out. A few kind villagers would give her food. She would take it stealthily and hurry back to her secret lair, that she changed often.

About an hour after our arrival, a young man came to inform us that they had spotted Devi on top of a haystack. We rushed to the spot. The hurried journey reminded me of our safari at the famous Masai Mara wild life park of Kenya. When word got around that there was a family of lions in a secluded corner of the park, our guide and driver rushed us to the spot at breakneck speed, lest we miss the sight.

My conscience was making me remorseful, since we were hurrying to catch a flesh and blood human being. We were worried too; she might disappear if we did not reach the spot urgently.

We did reach her and were shocked at what we saw. Atop a haystack was this frail and dishevelled woman, her clothes in tatters, who looked scared and hunted. She was trying to find a way out from the area. A few villagers with sticks in hand stood guard, preventing her escape. No amount of persuasion, cajoling and promise of a bribe in terms of delicious food could stir her out of her hiding place. Ultimately, two young men climbed up and overpowered her. They brought her down.

And good heavens! What a ghastly sight! She looked positively repelling. There she was, a frail and short woman, her hair knotted and flowing down from a small head like the props from the branches of an old banyan tree. There were lice in her hair. A pair of hollowed eyes, one of them injured, partially closed with streaks of blood oozing out, tattered clothes, unwashed for perhaps decades, the exposed skin layered with dust and grime and a horrific odour of urine, faeces and sweat emanated from her unwashed, untended parasite-infested body. She was trembling from head to toe with fear.

The first thing that Nilima did was to take her forcefully to a nearby well. There, assisted by two local women, Devi was given a thorough bath. The women repeatedly smeared the soap cake on her until some of the accumulated dirt and grime were washed out. The entire operation took about an hour. One of the women had arranged for some old, clean clothes, and helped her wear them. With clean clothes, she looked pretty decent, although her wet knotted hair still gave her a strange look. Thereafter we took her to the schoolteacher's house who gave her a heavy meal, which she devoured in a few moments. Finally, it was time for us to leave.

With some herbs smeared on her injured eye by the good schoolteacher, the bleeding stopped. Later on, we were told, someone tried to gorge out her eye to ward off her purported evil sight. The schoolteacher's intervention had stopped the ghastly act but as we discovered later, the damage to her eye was irreversible.

We forcibly took her to the car. However, all our efforts to persuade her to get in failed. We were informed that she had never been near a car in her life. So scared was she that when we managed to forcefully put her inside the car, she wet herself. We had to bring her down again, give her another bath and some used clean clothes. Finally, we pushed her in the car and started our return journey.

The three-hour ride back was uneventful, except that all along, Devi kept on holding the coat hanger so firmly, that we were worried her blue veins would burst. She trembled continuously. Her hands must have pained for days thereafter.

On reaching Seneh, our home for destitute old women, she jumped out as soon as the doors opened and started running towards the road. However, her cramped legs soon gave way and she slumped down like a dove with broken wings. Nilima was instantly there to help and reasoned with her in Nepalese not to panic.

The night was uneventful. She ate a hefty meal and slept like a log. Next morning, her hair was shaved off, and she was taught the use of a toilet. After a forced hot bath and new clothes, she looked clean and presentable. Nilima also tried to teach her how to wear clothes. (Although it has been nine years since, even today, she requires help to dress.)

After a couple of days, she was taken to an eye specialist who opined that her injured eye was lost forever. The other eye had cataract that has since been removed.

Initially, her stay was uneventful except for the quantity of food she ate. She would devour rice, lentils and vegetable–thrice the quantity a normal person is capable of having. Even then, she seemed unsatisfied. If we tried to restrict the quantity, she would lose her cool and throw the plate or any other item she could get hold of, at the person who was serving her. Another day, immediately after food, she went out in a huff and hit her own head hard with a brick. The wound sustained was so severe that it required five stitches. But this was not the end, rather it was the beginning of her violent acts of inflicting injuries on herself for the next seven days.

The villagers told us Devi would always behave in a deranged manner on full moon days and throw whatever she could get hold of at unsuspecting people, even without provocation. I remembered the scene out of an old Hollywood horror movie. As soon as the full moon was up in the sky, a fox would start howling and a blood-sucking ugly man would emerge in search of human prey. I fail to understand why some people believe full moon nights make people crazy.

Devi was taken to a psychiatrist, who immediately diagnosed her mental problems and prescribed regular medications to suppress her anxiety. It worked wonders. Within days, she became meek and quiet. Her craving for food also reduced. Since then, Devi has been a very lovable, petite, hunched and radiant woman, who speaks only when spoken to, never makes an issue of anything or ever complains. She remains in her own world, sitting and sleeping, always ready for a jig when asked, without any expression of joy or dismay on her face. She, however, continues to be on psychiatric drugs.

A few years back, we had a scare. After a brief illness,

she collapsed. Her blood pressure dropped to dangerously low limits, her oxygen level dropped alarmingly and she started gasping for breath. After initial medical intervention at Seneh, she was shifted to the Government Medical College Hospital. She was straightaway admitted to the ICU by the attending doctors at Emergency.

After a few days in the ICU, the doctors lost all hope. They decided to send her back to die in peace. ICU beds are always in great demand in a free government hospital. But we decided to give a last try and rushed her to a private hospital. There, the doctors wanted to put her on the ventilator. The cost involved was a matter of concern for a small organisation like ours. But we brushed it aside. And, lo and behold, after five days on life support, to the astonishment of all including the doctors, she started breathing normally and three days thereafter, she was discharged. She got a fresh lease of life. It was a miracle, the will of God, the doctors said.

Devi, about 95 now, is a symbol of our success, proof of the dedication of our supporting staff, and above all, a living example of life's triumphs over tribulations.

Arti Mandal

The Soul Yearns For Love And Order

'Ma, please, give me something to eat. I am very hungry,' said a sobbing Arjun, Arti's three-year-old youngest son.

'Wait, Dad should be coming home any moment now. He will bring rice from the shop at Kumrikata,' said Arti. Silently she prayed her husband would be a responsible father and bring the provisions. Her children had not eaten anything since morning.

The small town Kumrikata, where the nearest provision shop was located, was some three-odd kilometres away. Arti had given her husband the ten-rupee note she received from her employer as an advance from her current month's pay. Luckily for them, her husband had a half-day's work to finish in a nearby village, and with his earning for the day and Arti's money, he would have enough to buy rice and lentils to see them through seven days or so.

Normally, Arti avoided giving her husband any money. In fact, she would travel to his workplace at the end of the day to collect his wages. Out of this, she would give him a small sum to buy his drinks, without which he created a nuisance. But that afternoon, she could not leave the house because Rubi, their daughter, was running high fever. She knew her husband was very fond of Rubi, and at least for her, would come home early.

The unprecedented drought had made their lives extremely difficult. Because of the crop failure, the paddy harvest was almost half the normal produce. The landlord whose land they tilled on crop sharing basis, gave them more than their share out of pity but with six mouths to feed, the quantity was barely sufficient to last for eight months. To augment their earnings, her husband worked as a daily labourer in the non-farming season. In addition, Arti also worked as a part time help in wealthy households.

But the drought had made jobs difficult to find. In fact, the draught affected all—the poor and the relatively well-off alike, in the same way that flood waters spare none. In Arti's case, there was another scourge. Even if her husband did get a day's job, if Arti did not intervene, he would spend most part of his earnings on his drinking and gambling.

He had not been like that when they tied the knot eleven years back. She was only sixteen and he around twenty-two. Her father had fixed her marriage without her knowledge. According to the custom prevalent in their society, the bride had no right to decide for herself or even to meet the prospective groom before the marriage was solemnised. She was the eldest of the four siblings, the other three being boys. Her father was a marginal farmer who grew rice and vegetables in the small-scattered bits of land he owned.

The three coconut trees in their courtyard also produced a good harvest every year. They could also sell a small quantity of milk seasonally when more than one of the three cows they owned were lactating. Her mother was very hard working. She was blessed with robust health and supplemented their earnings by cooking household sweets on orders. Arti's job was to deliver them. Normally such orders would come at least once in a month. In addition, the mother was occasionally employed as a cook for feasts hosted by the wealthy. All in all, life was not difficult for the family.

From her early age, Arti accompanied her mother for such work, helping her cut and wash vegetables. Occasionally, she was asked to tend the wood fires on which the food was cooked. Arti's tender cheeks would flush pink whenever she stoked the fire but she always looked forward to such opportunities.

Arti suddenly remembered the day when a spark fell on her frock, and without her knowledge, the hem caught fire. When the fire burnt her thigh, she realised what had happened and started screaming. Her mother bravely doused the fire by patting it down with her bare hands and in the process, sustained minor burns herself. Arti's hand involuntarily travelled to the scar left behind by the burn.

Her mind flew back quickly to the days of her childhood. Being the only girl child in the family, her father and her two healthy brothers and their spouses had a special love and attachment for her. Even her mentally unsound brother (the villagers called him the lunatic one) always looked at her with a tenderness in his eyes, like a mother does to her newborn. This brother often disappeared for days, dishevelled and lost, and normally was found loitering on the streets of nearby villages muttering to himself and gesturing as if he was ordering the subjects of his imaginary kingdom. Whenever he came home, it was Arti who offered him food which he happily accepted. She was advised to stay away from him, since his behaviour was unpredictable. But quite often, stealthily, she went near him and patted him. He would laugh aloud in response, startling her.

'Ma, I am very hungry. Can I have something

even if it is not the usual meal time?' Arti's reverie was interrupted by her son's pleadings. She went to the kitchen and fetched three half-ripe bananas. That was the only food item left at home and she gave one each to the younger two, the third was to be shared by the elder two. Her eldest son gave his share away.

Suddenly, Arti's husband Mandal staggered in, fully drunk, talking to himself incoherently, his usual stammer coming in the way of finishing his sentences. He had a small polythene bag containing a little rice that was insufficient even for two meals.

Arti was livid with anger and frustration. She screamed at him and in a fit of rage, caught hold of his shirt collar and hit him repeatedly on his chest with her clenched fists. Her husband tried to ward off her blows and disentangle her grip but his steps were unstable. He fell on his back with a little push from Arti, who climbed atop him and continued hitting him, all the while howling in desperation.

Soon a spent force, she clung to Mandal, her husband, and started sobbing uncontrollably. Mandal also started crying with her. The children joined the chorus. When she had cooled down, she was bewildered by her violent outburst, and remorse and guilt seized her mind and body. She tenderly helped her husband to stand, like one does to a child after he falls on sand, and dusted off his tattered and soiled clothes.

Arti was endowed with robust health. She could work through the day. Fatigue was a word unknown to her. The moment she would lie down to sleep, she used to slump like dead wood, undisturbed even by dreams. But shortly after the incident, she started experiencing a strange phenomenon. As soon as she lay down to sleep, her mind would start revolving in circles. Incoherent and inscrutable thoughts crept into her mind. Sleep deserted her. She woke up exhausted and confused. Her mind became foggy and edgy. She would snap like a dog prodded with a stick.

Unfortunately, the children became the main victims of her unexplained mood swings. They got beaten up on the slightest pretext.

Days went by in hardship and turmoil. The husband became elusive and withdrawn, spending more time away from home. The children started dreading their mother and tried to keep away from her out of fear. The only one who even then could steal some affection from her, was her youngest son, who was three-and-a-half years old.

The final blow came when Arti forgot where she had left her youngest toddler in the crowded weekly market. The unfortunate child could not be traced, no matter how much they searched. The loss devastated her completely. And, with the loss of her child, Arti lost her mind completely and became a victim of violent schizophrenia. Unable to bear the trauma of a schizophrenic wife and the howls of the starving children, Arti's husband hanged himself from a wooden bridge. When the villagers brought his dead body to their courtyard, Arti stared at him for long without batting an eyelid till her eyes got red shot, and then, she started laughing loudly.

Suddenly, she pulled out a bamboo pole and started chasing the crowd that had assembled around her house. She was intent on hitting whoever came her way. The crowd ran helter-skelter but she kept chasing them. A dog came in her way. She hit its head so hard that the poor creature's head split into two. The children locked themselves inside the house and started howling in absolute fear. She tried to break open the door. However, suddenly, both her brothers and brother-in law pounced on her, and after a lot of struggle, overpowered her.

That was the beginning of the end of Arti's normal family life till I met her at a remote village near Kumrikata, around 300 km from Guwahati, the capital of Assam. We went there to rescue Devi, whose life I portrayed in the previous chapter. This was in August 2011.

Neatly dressed and behaving normally, Arti insisted I take her along with Devi. She told me no one liked her in the village and made fun of her. I checked from the villagers who informed me that Arti hailed from a nearby village. She lived alone although she had three children. At least twice in a month, almost at regular intervals, Arti would lose her mind and behave like a possessed woman, extremely abusive and violent. No one dared to go near her in that period. She hurled whatever she could get hold of, at anyone who ventured near her.

Normally her brother, with help, would skilfully overpower her and tie her to a tree in their courtyard. In such a delirious state, she refused to eat or drink for days and remained awake hurling filthy abuses to all and sundry. She did not sleep a wink. Normally in about a week's time, completely exhausted and spent, and absolutely dissipated, she would fall asleep like deadwood, standing and tied to the tree. When she would finally wake up, she was a normal person again.

When in a trance, the worst victims of her strange behaviour were her children. The very sight of them would infuriate her. So terrified were the children, they were scared to approach her even when she was normal. Their maternal grandmother, a widow, had taken them to her house and they lived with her. The mother visited Arti regularly and gave her food when she was normal. The children always kept away.

We summoned her mother, a sixty-year-old sprightly lady who with folded hands appealed to us to take Arti along and try to help her. Arti came happily, like a child when given a new toy. When we reached our home for destitute old women, she behaved like a newborn calf, happy and energetic, running about from one room to the other and smiling with gusto.

For a good ten days, she was a very well-behaved energetic woman, who sang and laughed with the others and helped them in keeping the surroundings clean. She took part in all the activities like a disciplined soldier and assimilated perfectly with the environment. Then one morning, she got up from bed with eyes as red as burning charcoals. Her roommates told me she had not slept the entire night. She kept talking to herself. A number of times, she came out of the room and kept pacing the long verandah. To be fair to her, she made efforts not to disturb the others. The entire day, she kept on talking to herself and walked around with vigorous strides, paying no heed to what was happening around her.

She, however, had her meals properly. The doctor gave her heavy sedation that evening, but she did not close her eyes even once. As a matter of abundant caution, she was shifted to a vacant room and the nurse and help boy were instructed to keep an eye on her the whole night. They noticed that in the wee hours, she became restless and started banging the door even though it was kept unlocked.

During the day, she became extremely restless and abusive. Her eyes turned ferocious, and she paced around like a tigress ready to pounce on her prey. In addition, she started spewing venom to all and sundry without provocation. She appeared so dangerous that no one dared to go near her. Very cautiously, I approached her with a glass of water and called her name softly and tenderly. She stared at me for a long time and without any sign of aggression, she accepted the glass and drank the water. I asked for a banana and gave it to her. She ate that too without protest. That was the beginning of our father-daughter relationship which probably was instrumental in bringing normalcy to her life.

For a good seven days or more, she could not sleep a wink despite the heavy sedation–both oral and intravenous that was given to her. All those days, she ate just one or two bananas. Almost all along, she remained disturbed and agitated, her eyes red hot, her hair loose and flowing all over like the mane of a lion on the run. All twenty-four hours of the day, she kept pacing around like a hyena in a cage. She never looked tired or spent. Luckily for us, except for a solitary instance of her throwing a stone at another resident, she did not resort to any physical violence.

On the seventh day, completely dissipated of any energy, she slumped on the bench kept on the verandah. And instantly dosed off. After a while, her limp body was lifted and placed on her bed. She slept for a good eighteen hours and woke up dazed, as if her slumber had been disturbed by a dream full of horror. She then washed herself without help and ate a robust meal. She remembered nothing of what had happened in the last seven days. We never allowed anyone to talk about it either. Arti then became her normal self, ebullient, hardworking and courteous.

She was absolutely normal for the next thirteen days, when once again she started behaving abnormally. In between, we had checked with a psychiatrist who had advised us to hospitalise her in a psychiatric hospital if the attacks resurfaced. We had already spoken to Dr Anjana Goswami, founder-chairman of Ashadeep, an NGO providing yeoman service to the mentally sick. She agreed to treat her free in their psychiatric hospital. So, when she started showing signs of an imminent attack, we took her to their hospital and admitted her there.

She remained in the hospital for almost a year. I visited her at regular intervals. As her treatment progressed, gradually, her physical health deteriorated to the point when she was like a skeleton, her long hair was cropped and clean, giving prominence to her hollow and lost eyes. Whenever she saw me, she would trot out like a baby, hug my legs, cry aloud in joy and appeal to me to take her back. She would then call a few other inmates, introduce me to them as her adopted father and with her own hands, distribute the sweets that I made it a habit to take along. The parting was always heart-wrenching, as she wouldn't let go of me easily.

After thirteen months, we were allowed to bring her back as she was declared cured. However, there was a rider. She would need regular psychiatric medication for life and we were advised to keep her away from any mental shock.

It took us a good six months to bring Arti back to shape. Her health improved, and she became radiant, energetic and happy.

We decided the time had come to gradually reunite her with her family. We first got her mother to visit her. That venerable old lady could not believe her eyes. Seeing her mother, Arti ran to her, gave her a passionate bear hug and suddenly burst out crying. So did the mother. They continued to hug and hold each other for the next twenty minutes.

The mother stayed back for the night; they slept on the same bed and talked through the night. The next morning, the mother left with the promise that she would come within a couple of weeks with Arti's youngest son.

The mother kept her promise and came back with the son who was now around eight. Seeing her dear son, Arti rushed to him with open arms, but the child ran away from her in utter panic. No amount of persuasion could make him come to the mother. We made the grandmother-grandson duo stay back for the night. When the unsuspecting boy was fast asleep, we shifted him to Arti's bed.

The ruse worked. The next morning, the boy woke up in Arti's lap. He stared long and hard at Arti and suddenly embraced her and clung to her, bringing tears to our eyes. We made him stay back for a few days. The old lady was sent back to fetch the other children. For all the three days, the mother-son duo was inseparable. In three days, the old lady came back with Arti's twelve-year-old daughter.

The reunion was eventless except that all along, Arti's tears kept rolling down as if she had held them back for just this occasion. On the third day, Arti's fifteen-year-old eldest son also arrived. He was now a fully grown lad with a lot of composure who did not betray any emotion. We provided a separate room for the entire family to stay together. All along, the support staff kept a hawk's eye on Arti.

After a day, the family left. We called them back on the fifth day and when all the children departed, Arti was morose and withdrawn for the next two days.

It was decided that the children would continue staying with their grandmother. The eldest got an apprenticeship job as a scooter mechanic and started living in the shop. We sent Arti home for four days to spend time with her family. The nurse was also sent along as a precaution. Honestly, we wanted to send Arti back permanently, but the mother appealed to us with folded hands to keep Arti with us. We reluctantly obliged. It appeared she had a premonition about what was in store. We also ensured the younger children went to school in their village.

In between, Arti went home twice; once to spend a week with her children and on another occasion, to attend the marriage of her youngest brother. We explained to her how important it was for her to have the medication regularly and that she was to look after her medication herself, without fail.

One day, we received a message that her mother had suffered cardiac arrest and died. Arti was escorted back to her village and she stayed there for ten days without any external help.

Later, we rehabilitated the boys. We could get the eldest son a job as a scooter mechanic in a not so far-off place. We organised admission of her other son in a boarding school near Guwahati run by an NGO. Unfortunately, we failed to rehabilitate her adolescent daughter. She had hardly attended school and because of her vulnerable age, we were cautious in finding a proper place for her. Her maternal uncle, who runs a small business, undertook to keep her with him. After a few months, we found a place for her through the good office of the Chairman of the State Child Welfare Board. When our representative went to fetch her, the girl refused to leave her uncle. The uncle and the aunt also protested. They came back empty-handed.

At that time, little did we imagine the reprehensibly evil design of the greedy, rapacious uncle. Without our knowledge, the poor child was married off to a widower thirty years her elder. He had a daughter from his earlier marriage who was of the same age as his young wife. I heard a large sum had changed hands. By the time we came to know about the ugly union, it was too late as the fourteen-year-old was already pregnant. Later, we came to know, Arti knew about it all along but kept it a secret. Probably her ailing mind did not understand the import. And alas! when after the full term, she heard about the birth of her grandson, her happiness knew no bounds. She laughed and hummed in absolute happiness.

Arti today is a bubble of energy. Clean and suave, steady, cool and ever-smiling. She exudes confidence and is endowed with robust health.

Sukhi'

A Lost Childhood

Deep inside a network of grime-filled alleys was a small shanty. It had an old corrugated iron roof top with black polythene sheets under it, to keep the rains at arm's length. The walls were made of bamboo strips and hessian. There, with her parents and three siblings, lived Sukhi, a six-year-old who was partially hearing and speech impaired. Their neighbours remembered her as a child born partially deaf and dumb, who could make others of her age follow her in the kind of childhood activities that six-year-olds indulge in.

With her broad shoulders, plump body, long, pointed face and irregularly cropped hair, Sukhi looked more like a teen tomboy. Her jaw line was even, with glittering teeth, two front ones missing, and heavy lips. Her light copper-coloured bare body, tanned by the scorching sun, was smooth and soft like satin. The most striking feature of her face was her blackish-grey eyes, large and deep-set, the eyelashes fluttering regularly like the wings of a butterfly and the eyebrows thick and curving, like the third day's moon.

In the cluster, Sukhi, undoubtedly, was the healthiest child, always jumping and bouncing around like a ping-pong ball.

Sukhi's parents were poor, in fact, very poor. Her father was an alcoholic. Her mother worked as a daily labourer on construction sites to feed the family. Sukhi was very scared of her father, who would quarrel frequently with her mother and beat her up mercilessly if she refused to part with her hard-earned money for his drinking sprees. Sukhi never forgot the almost fatal shove her drunk father gave her on that fateful evening, when she tried to save her mother from his beatings.

She was only nine then. It resulted in her head falling like a dry coconut on a brick. When she regained consciousness, she found her mother crying near her bed. Her head was throbbing and reeling. She remained confined to the bed for the next fifteen days with her head bandaged and her wounds smeared with some medicinal herbs. She became partially deaf and dumb due to the damage done.

Her father did try to make amends but she rebuffed his advances resolutely. She never shed tears when he died three years later of cirrhosis of the liver. Post her head injury, she constantly complained of severe headaches and soon started having delusions of her father's ghost stalking her whenever she walked alone on the road.

Despite this and their poverty, after her father's death, the next three years were relatively peaceful. In those days, it was her duty to do the household chores fetch water, clean the shack they lived in, wash clothes in the nearby rivulet, keep a motherly watch on her younger siblings, and cook the rice with the potatoes for lunch, while her mother went to work.

By the time she was fifteen, her mother decided that Sukhi too needed to go to work with her. So, Sukhi's eleven-year-old younger sibling stepped into her shoes, while both mother and daughter worked. With their combined earnings, they were able to add a broth of lentils to their daily meals of rice and salted, mashed potatoes; once in a while, they even ate some fish. Their joy knew no bounds when, one evening, her mother bought a small transistor from the local market. The next day, the mother-daughter duo did not go to work and the family spent all the time together listening to the songs emanating from the transistor. Sukhi partially heard some of the songs and was able to gyrate to the rhythm. That day, they probably had the best meal of their life, consisting of rice, fish curry, *Muri Ghanto* (a spicy dish made out of large fish heads), and a tomato *tak*, a sweet chutney of tomatoes.

By sixteen, Sukhi turned out to be a very attractive woman. In spite of her repeated, almost involuntary, attempts to hide her large chest with her nylon sari, she could always feel the hungry gaze of her male co-workers penetrating her. Whenever she walked with her confident gait, her perfectly rounded hips swayed like a swan's. Her waist was very slim compared to her broad shoulders, the stomach flat and smooth, the skin flawless light copper, the small but deep canal linking her nose to her upper lip giving her long nose even more prominence. Her sensuality was the envy of all her peers at her workplace as well as in the cluster of shanties they lived in. Her robust health added to her charm.

She was proud of her attributes, little knowing that they would be the major cause of her tribulations in later life. Notwithstanding her handicaps, there was no dearth of admirers and suitors. The overseer of the daily work force where Sukhi and her mother worked, always showed unusual interest in Sukhi, ensuring that she and her mother were given lighter jobs.

He was a young man of about thirty, tall and muscular with a pencil thin whisker separated by a thick growth in the middle intentionally kept unshaved but trimmed. It looked like a bow with a flat arrowhead with the long mouth looking like the string. His long hair that hung neatly over the ears, was oiled and parted in the middle. His wheatish complexion, lips always red with the saliva generated by the constant chewing of *paan*, and his authoritarian demeanour gave him a strange attractiveness. His small piercing eyes invariably travelled over Sukhi's body. His name was Viru and everyone called him Viru Dada.

His office was a shed with a cast iron as roof, all four sides open, with a small table and two rickety chairs in one corner. He did all the book-keeping work perched cross-legged on one chair, with the other chair placed on the opposite side. He maintained the thick broad register and kept accounts of all the labourers. Occasionally, he would walk around to supervise the work and invariably shout at labourers who were slow and weak or found resting a little too often.

At the end of the day, each labourer would file past him, first the women and next, the men, and he would pay each the day's wage. The women labourers would get Rs 50 and the men Rs 70 each. Each one was required to first sign the receipt in the column kept for the purpose against their names before the day's wage was handed over. Since almost all of them were illiterate, their left hand thumb impressions were affixed on the column in lieu of signatures. Normally, he would hold the thumb of each, rub it on the ink pad, and press the thumb in the right place so that it did not spill into the next block. In the case of Sukhi, he would be very tender, hold her hand longer than essential and gently squeezed her hand before he let it go. Sukhi hated it.

Sukhi never forgot the wet day of October, when she came for work alone as her mother was sick. The sky was overcast, with heavy to light showers bringing down the temperature. The attendance was thin because of the rains. Sukhi was drenched to the skin, her wet sari clinging to her, revealing the contours of her body. Viru Dada's eyes glittered like a hungry cat when he saw Sukhi. He entrusted her with the job of mopping the newly laid floor of a room located on the third floor. All the other labourers were given work on the first floor.

During the lunch break, it was customary for the labourers to take rest after their meals for a short while before the post lunch work started. Being partially deaf and dumb, Sukhi rarely communicated with the others apart from her mother. That afternoon, after lunch, she lay down flat on her back and dozed off. Suddenly, she had a feeling someone was standing near her. She opened her eyes to find Viru there. He looked at her eyes and then his gaze slipped down her body.

From the movement of his lips, Sukhi knew that he was gazing at her with desire. He winked at her, closed the door and tried to force himself on Sukhi. She, in turn, mustered all her strength to fend off his advances, and tried to shriek, but other than a choked gurgle and some almost inaudible groans of pain and despair, no sound came out of her mouth. Later, completely violated both physically and mentally, Sukhi staggered back home in tears.

That one incident changed her life forever.

Two and a half months later, Sukhi did not go for work. In sign language, she told her mother that she was feeling terribly sick in her stomach. When the next day also, Sukhi did not get up from her bed and complained of nausea, her mother recognised the early symptoms of pregnancy. The mother was livid. She shrieked and cried aloud and started hitting Sukhi mercilessly. Not knowing the reasons for their mother's anguish, the other children started crying, too.

Hearing the commotion, the neighbours also trooped in and a few women physically prevented the mother from assaulting Sukhi. When relative calm was restored, and the mother-daughter duo refused to let them know the reason for the upheaval, Sukhi once again had a bout of nausea. The shrewd ones immediately guessed the reason. Ultimately, Sukhi relented and told her mother of how the overseer had taken advantage of her. Some of the neighbours blamed the mother for allowing the daughter to go to work alone. But a majority of them decided Viru Dada needed to pay for his actions. After prolonged deliberations, it was agreed that a delegation accompanied by Sukhi and her mother will go to the police to lodge a complaint.

Viru Dada was an active member of the youth wing of the ruling party. Their complaint went unheeded. The people were scared of the clout that Viru Dada wielded in the area. Everyone knew that Viru Dada could walk free even if he committed a murder.

Initially, the Sub Inspector on duty at the police station refused to lodge a First Information Report. After ardent pleading and negotiations about the bribe to be paid, he agreed to lodge the FIR. But while taking down Sukhi's statement that was being converted to words from her sign language by her mother, his pen stopped suddenly as soon as the name of Viru Dada cropped up. He could not dare to lodge a FIR against a member of the youth wing of the ruling party. He advised Sukhi's mother to terminate the pregnancy and keep quiet. But the assembly refused to relent. They all marched to the construction site to confront Viru Dada.

The police, in the meantime, despatched a runner to Viru to forewarn him about the impending confrontation, who, therefore, had his battle plans ready when the agitated group reached him. He waited for them coolly. The group confronted him about his utterly despicable, dastardly and unpardonable conduct of taking advantage of a vulnerable deaf and partially dumb girl. They demanded that he not only publicly apologise to them, but also promise to marry Sukhi and make her his legally wedded wife. Otherwise, they threatened, he would face dire consequences of their wrath. Someone in the group shouted that he would not only be maimed, but also castrated.

Viru was cool and calm like a fallen leaf in a bucket full of still water. He feigned absolute ignorance about what they were saying. He swore repeatedly about his innocence. When he found that the irate mob would not be appeased, he mumbled, 'Well, it is not my habit or duty, to spy on the personal lives of the workers or speak about it. I would not have uttered a word about what I saw on a rainy day on the third floor. But now that you people have pointed a finger at me, a devout family man with a loving wife and a toddler son, I will tell you what I saw'.

He waited a bit to gauge their response. When he found them finally listening, he continued, 'First, I apologise to Sukhi, as against my principles, I am breaking the promise I made to her and Ramu.'

Ramu had the reputation of being a loose cannon and was a habitual alcoholic, who, if not completely sozzled, would come to work and pass lewd remarks about his women peers that invariably resulted in verbal duels and at times, scuffles. The other workers hated him. But Viru had a soft corner for him for a special reason. He was ever ready to put his thumb impressions wherever Viru wanted, even against his own name, post facto, on days when he was absent. The money generated as wages on such occasions was pocketed by Viru Dada. Ramu received a bottle of cheap country liquor as a reward.

Viru continued, 'Give me a few minutes. I will be embarrassed if I am to narrate the scene in graphic details. I will get Ramu. You can ask him directly what happened that afternoon.' He ordered two of his trusted labourers to fetch Ramu.

Soon after, Ramu came staggering in, supported by the two, blabbering incoherently. The two escorts took him directly to where Sukhi stood. She did not hear what Viru was saying, but as soon as Ramu was produced and deliberately made to stand by her side, she immediately understood Viru's gameplan. For a very long time, she stared at Viru and then at Ramu. Suddenly, her eyes turned wild, she glared at Viru like a wounded tigress and in a fit of rage, ran towards a heap of bricks, picked up one, and with lightning speed, planted a heavy blow on Viru's skull, cracking it.

Then Sukhi ran and ran, all along she felt being stalked by her father's ghost, till she could remember nothing....

Sukhi was spotted loitering aimlessly at Pan Bazar, Guwahati. According to the volunteers of Ashadeep, an NGO taking care of the mentally sick who had rescued her, she used to crisscross the streets and alleys of Pan Bazar, absolutely oblivious of the world around her, wearing ragged and soiled clothes, sleeping on a street corner even when it was raining without any shelter to protect her. She ate whatever shopkeepers or pedestrians in the area gave her. She was dirty, her looks were forlorn, somewhat wild but she was absolutely harmless, living in her own world of fantasy. She continuously indulged in conversations with herself.

Ashadeep had brought her to their shelter on 4 November 2005. She was admitted to their psychiatric hospital and put on drugs. She took an inordinately long time to come to terms with her surroundings. At times, she displayed mildly violent behaviour, but otherwise, she was a very obedient patient. After seven years, she finally showed signs of recovery. They put her on rehab, but she was unable to adjust fully to her surroundings and they did not know how and where to rehabilitate her.

They finally informed me about her and I undertook to look after her at Seneh. When she came to us on 28 March 2012, she was thin, like a straw, her hair in knots and completely full of parasites. Her teeth were decayed and she was very slow in responding to questions or advice. She had a very poor appetite and slept for the entire day. Her nights were disturbed and restless.

On her arrival, the first thing that Nilima, our hard-working nurse, did, was to bathe her thoroughly and then cut short her unruly hair. With new clothes, she looked relatively decent. When Dr Kalpana Bora, our ever-inspiring septuagenarian voluntary doctor examined her, she found Sukhi had very high blood pressure and several other health issues. She was put on medication right away.

Within a couple of weeks, we got Sukhi's entire teeth extracted in four or five sittings, and after a month, provided her with a pair of dentures. It was a lovely sight to see Sukhi smiling like a baby after she first got her dentures. We arranged for an ENT specialist to examine her ears and provided her with a hearing aid, which she has been steadfastly refusing to wear.

Today, thanks to the efforts of everyone in Seneh, Sukhi is a very happy woman. She is and will be on lifelong psychiatric drugs. She has put on weight and is now very finicky about the cleanliness of the clothes she wears. She takes part in all the activities including cleaning the area, swabbing the floors and helping others do the cooking, besides cutting the vegetables and washing utensils. She is always ready for a jig when the Bihu song is played, and makes wonderful paper flowers.

Whenever I approach her, I habitually pat her cheeks and ask her about her well-being. Invariably, she complains about her health and about pain in her feet. Once, one of her toe nails got severed when she accidently stumbled on a stone. When attending to her injury, we noticed few of her toes were crooked. A doctor later explained that the reason for that was long-neglected arthritis.

I felt deeply hurt. Poor Sukhi had been complaining to us about pain in her legs, but we never took her seriously.

We thought it is natural at her age; with advancing age, I too have been experiencing unexplained pains all over my body. I always remember a Russian friend who told me about a saying in his country, which translated into English, reads: 'If any one does not complain about pain after fifty, he has to be a dead man.' Sukhi's pains, it turned out, were for a different reason altogether.

Author's Note: The entire episode narrated in the earlier part of the chapter is a work of pure fiction. I could not trace any verifiable evidence, whatsoever, to link it to Sukhi's past. We know nothing about her past, nor about her antecedents. Even the name, Sukhi, by which we call her, because she is always happy, is not her real name.

Sukhi remembers nothing about her past. Unlike all of us, lesser mortals, Sukhi lives for today, dances whenever asked to do so, constantly complains of a headache or some other pain, and dresses up elegantly, the way she has been taught at Seneh. She washes her own clothes including the bedspreads, and unlike a few others, maintains a reasonable standard of personal hygiene. Above all, she shows real compassion for Sarala, a visually impaired co-resident. It is a heartening sight to see Sukhi always leading Sarala around, holding her hand and guiding her at all times.

In putting together this story, I took the following cues and circumstantial evidences:

I researched the causes for onset of schizophrenia by reading a few papers published by renowned psychiatrists. Some of the reasons, they said, include:

a. Genetics
b. Environmental factors
c. Internal brain structure
d. Head injury
e. Sexual and physical abuse in early years
f. Delusions

I manipulated some of these reasons as the cause for Sukhi's mental problems. Similarly, while asleep, even today, Sukhi invariably keeps murmuring continuously audible but illegible words. This could suggest that she was abused in childhood.

While we have not been able to find out where Sukhi hailed from, we know she is a Bengali since she responds better when spoken to in that language. At times, Sukhi suddenly expresses a desire to go home by train to meet her daughter. When we ask her the name of the place she wants to go, or the name of her sister, she gives a blank look.

Hence, I imagined Siliguri as the place of her birth–it is easily accessible by train from Guwahati.

Once an electrician resembling the description of Viru Dada came to Seneh for some repairs. Sukhi was visibly agitated, she started hurling abuses at the man for no rhyme or reason. We never saw her so agitated ever.

Later when she was asked why she hated the poor man, she said he is an evil person. Viru Dada's part in her story was imagined from this episode.

Bina

Does The Past Matter?

Although it is almost eight years since Bina came into the Seneh family, even today, we have no clue about who she was, where she came from or what her name was before she came to us. I debated in my mind whether I should include her story in the book. I decided in the affirmative because she is such a darling of a woman that, if not her past, then definitely her present needs portrayal. I leave it to the esteemed reader to judge if I have done justice to her story. In her case, I decided not to allow my imaginations to run riot, as I had done in a few cases I have penned earlier. But most of the profiles I had done earlier were based on some clues around which I could construct their lives. But for Bina, there were no clues, whatsoever.

Suffice it to say, Bina is one of the most likeable residents of Seneh with her ever-present grin dancing merrily on her heavy lips at all times. And the icing on the cake: she is extremely courteous and demure. But before I embark upon writing about the present-day Bina, let me admit that the name 'Bina' was my brain child, and it has survived for eight long years now. Two reasons prompted me to christen her Bina. First and foremost, her soft, cuckoo-like, musical voice. It resonates on the ears like the sound of a Veena (Bina in Assamese), a traditional musical string instrument that adorns the hands of Saraswati, the Goddess of learning in Hindu mythology. Next is her build. Her head is big and the shoulders broad. When you look at her standing quietly in a corner, it appears as if her body gradually tapers down. This is so because while standing, her legs and heels touch each other like a soldier standing in attention. The nearest analogy of her standing posture, I thought, was the Veena.

Now let us dwell on her grin. When she smiles her omnipresent smile, the lips part slightly, the upper one a little more than the lower, as if the muscles on her chin are unable to bear the weight of the lower heavier lip when parted. An alternative thought that may dawn on you; the muscles are conspiring to find ways and means to prevent movement of her comparatively less succulent dry lower lip. Her upper lip, on the other hand, does not face much of a resistance. The muscles under her nose cave in, making room for its upward movement. These muscles have managed an everlasting friendship and understanding with the adjoining cheek muscles. They allow formation of two perfect dimples right on the area where the ends of her jaw meet her cheeks, thereby allowing unrestricted movement of the upper lip. Her plump, healthy childlike cheeks make her dimples look even more prominent. The movement also exposes a partially decayed black-capped tooth.

Bina is a cleanliness freak and a human vacuum cleaner in action throughout the day. She roams around the Seneh campus like a cat—soundless and alert, ears raised, eyes roving, whiskers taut, prying, sniffing for a mouse. Bina moves around stealthily, prying for rags, used plastic bottles, plastic cups, torn papers, even some dried leaves blown in by the breeze. The moment her eyes fall on such objects of no consequence, she scoops them up and throws them straightaway into the garbage bin.

Perhaps you should drop by at Seneh to catch Bina in action. As a normal courtesy, the management ensures, within a couple of minutes of your being seated, that you are served a steaming hot black cup of tea in a paper tumbler and some light snacks by one of the residents with downcast eyes. Rest assured, there will be someone standing stealthily behind you, or at the door, keeping an eagle's eye on whatever is happening at the table.

Her vigil is not to spy on what you are doing, eating or talking. Her attention is on the table. Once again, do not be mistaken, for, she is not interested in knowing what you are doing with the helpings. Her entire attention is focused on when you empty the contents of your cup or decide to abandon it half way. The moment you put down your empty plate or your tumbler, she will swoop upon them, like a kite swooping down on its prey. She will then whisk it away and head briskly and triumphantly towards the disposal bin.

Her daily routine at Seneh starts with her habit of waking up long before the others are up or have even given their first yawn. By 6.30 am, she is ready in a clean fresh dress, with a generous application of oil on her grey-black hair, that gleams on the neatly combed hair tied together with a pony tail of sorts. Her signature grin starts hanging on her lips from that moment on. Without wasting time, she begins her daily morning routine.

She walks silently and slowly, shuffling her legs in small, firm steps, her eyes fixed on the courtyard she is crisscrossing, resembling a leopard approaching a doe. And as soon as she spots her prey, which is usually litter of any kind, she swoops down upon it and consigns it to the dustbin.

The garbage truck arrives around 8 am. Bina is ready, waiting on the roadside, with the day's garbage neatly tied in black polythene bags.

Like a heavyweight lifter, Bina lifts the bag above her head with ease, and tosses it into the open garbage hold of the truck, and '*plong*', the bag finds its place inside the hold. The pickup boys love Bina and call her *Zabar Aita* (Garbage Grandma). If for some pressing reason, she is unable to do the routine, the boys are alarmed and ask about her welfare. All along the entire operation, Bina maintains a stoic silence. And, when the truck departs, she returns with a sombre expression, her sari tucked into her waist, hands clasped behind her back, invariably muttering to herself.

Ask Bina a question, and her reply is always in monosyllables. In case she chooses to elongate her words into a sentence, it comes out in the voice of a child, timid and soft. You have to strain your ears a bit to understand what she is saying. It seems her tongue darts here and there, unable to make the right sound. As a consequence, you may mistake a 'lord' as 'oode 'or 'torn' as 'ton'. Honestly, it is music that she spits out with her words.

She looks as if she is the most contented person living on earth: cool, measured like a snail, and always unruffled. I felt that even the two most banal emotions, anger and anguished pain, can never ruffle her. But this impression was thrown to the wolves when one of the residents who shared her room breathed her last a couple of years ago. As soon as the lifeless body was brought home from the hospital before she was carried away to be cremated, Bina fell on her lifeless body, howling like a child, tears flowing in torrents down her puffy cheeks. Her hands had to be literally extricated by force from the limp body.

She lost her cool once again in another incident. One of her roommates, a kleptomaniac, stole from under her mattress, a sum of eight rupees that she had saved from the fifty rupees that we gave to each resident when they were taken on a guided tour of a few Durga Puja *mandaps.* Bina's rage was uncontrollable. It took some effort to stop her from inflicting injuries on the perpetrator. Bina tried to hit the poor woman with a raised chair. Surely, if the chair had landed on the frail body of the unfortunate kleptomaniac, she would have been grievously injured. Timely intervention saved the day. Other than these two incidents, Bina has not been known to even raise a finger at anyone. Once a rat nibbled at her toe while she was relaxing. She simply brushed it aside without any desire for vengeance. Similarly, when a Perrier dog dirtied her clothes as they lay drying on the grass, she even refrained from shooing the dog away, accepting his act as a *fait accompli.*

Sitting idle at one place for more than a few minutes is not in Bina's blood. For the entire duration of the daylight hours, Bina is constantly on the move. Her gait is that of a philosopher in deep thought. With her hands clasped at the back, she walks untiringly till fatigue forces her to sit on the armchair kept on the veranda by sunset.

She then dozes off occasionally. But when dinner is announced by ringing the bell kept for the purpose, she jumps up and is always the first to reach the dining area. Because Bina cannot be confined to any one place for more than a couple of minutes, by force of circumstance, she is allowed to skip the morning and evening prayer sessions, which are otherwise compulsory for all.

Bina also acts as the post-lunch dish washing machine. She almost regularly volunteers to wash all the common dishes and utensils left for cleaning after everyone completes their lunch. Naturally, other residents who are required to do the dishes by turn try to take advantage. Our staff ensures she is not over-exploited. On the other hand, post dinner, she hurries to her bed, unmindful of others, and before others have even finished eating, she will be snoring loudly, long before the cleaning up operations in the pantry even begin.

To sum up, Bina is a harmless, expressionless loner. She has a philosophical aloofness from all things material, has no cravings, no attachments, no likes or dislikes, no friend or enemy. She lives in her own world, and to me and to the others who know her, she is a darling of a woman, who lives deep within her cocoon. No outside influences can pollute or even touch her. She lives for today, tomorrow being of no consequence. And fittingly, her yesterdays are buried deep in some unknown location. She is at peace with herself. What a beautiful mind the sad happenings of her unknown past have bestowed on her! If all human beings are like her, this world would be a sublime place to live in.

Now let me dwell on whatever little I know about Bina and her past. I have an extraordinary, remarkable friend, Padma Shri Mukul Goswami. He gave up his lucrative banking job a decade ago to take up the cause of the mentally sick. He has dedicated his life for their welfare. He has built up from scratch a vibrant NGO by the name Ashadeep, and today, this NGO is giving succour to thousands of mentally sick people across the North East. His special focus is women. Thanks to his efforts, unlike other states, in Assam and neighbouring states, you hardly see any mentally sick woman loitering on the streets.

Bina was one of the first such women whom his organisation picked up from a street corner of a small town about 100 km from Guwahati. He treated her for her mental health issues in the psychiatric hospital he had started in a rented accommodation in Guwahati. After long hospitalisation, Bina recovered to a large extent. She became capable of living a normal life, provided she got adequate care and support. He tried his best to find someone remotely connected to Bina for rehabilitation. He was unsuccessful and failed to establish Bina's origins. On her part, she clearly didn't have any memory of her past.

Ashadeep soon had four patients who were cured like

Bina. It became a huge challenge for him. They urgently required a home full of understanding and compassion to ensure that their unfortunate maladies do not resurface. I volunteered to take some load off his overburdened shoulders. He along with the psychiatrist who had treated the four women emphasised that what Bina and the other women required was an understanding environment so that gradually and cautiously, they were brought back to the mainstream social order. The doctor also emphasised that any disruption in the treatment regime that they required on a daily basis for the rest of their lives, may lead to a recurrence of their problems. I was moved by what they had achieved and their commitment. I promised that Seneh would do its best.

Bina became a resident of Seneh along with two others of her kind almost eight years ago. Sukhi, whose life I tried to depict earlier (based more on fiction and circumstantial evidence), was another one of them. The third, a fifty-plus unfortunate woman with an imposing figure, tall and sharp-featured, gradually started behaving oddly after six months. She had to be sent back for readmission in the hospital. I am not aware about her present condition.

Sukhi and Bina are the quietest, gentlest and friendliest of all the inhabitants of Seneh who have chosen (by compulsion or design) to make it their home for the rest of their lives. The residents are all from different backgrounds. Hence occasional squabbles, defiance of orders, and wilful deviation from routine are an everyday affair that our staff face.

At times, controlling a select few of them to bring order becomes a challenge. But the two most docile non-troubling residents of Seneh for the last eight years are these two wonderful human beings, Sukhi and Bina. To the best of my knowledge, they have not once created issues or irritated anyone, residents and support staff alike. They are like two lovable babies. And the most endearing of all their qualities are their all-encompassing smiles that rarely leave their lips. Astonishingly, they are among the healthiest with hardly any health issues of note. And both are bundles of energy.

Late Sadhana Bora

A Mother Whom No One Wanted

It was one of those rare cloudless days of the rainy season. To be specific, it was the evening of 12 July 2016. The red rays of the setting sun gradually turned golden, taking on a coppery hue as the end of the day drew near. The reflection of the setting sun could be seen majestically fading into the bed of the Brahmaputra river, which flows with its full foam and fury parallel to the Boothnath Crematorium in Guwahati. The amber-coloured rays of the setting sun fell on the face of Sadhana Bora's lifeless body, kept atop her funeral pyre, just before the logs were placed over her body to light the pyre according to Hindu tradition. The rays lent a certain serenity to her face that was never seen when she was alive. She seemed bathed in peace and tranquillity. Gone were the marks of turmoil and despair that overshadowed her face when she was alive.

I was saddened and remorseful that I had mistaken those frowns as the manifestation of some mental disorder.

Standing beside the pyre, looking at the serene and peaceful face of the corpse, I felt agitated. How can men be so selfish, ruthless and cruel? How can society turn a blind eye to what is happening in the vicinity? Are we mere pawns in the hands of our materialistic natures, forgetting that we, as a species, are supposed to be superior because of our intellect, and our ability to love and be compassionate?

With each log placed on top of her lifeless body, I realised the futility of wealth and material pleasures, for when the end comes, everyone is reduced to a lifeless heap, a corpse which must be either buried, burnt to ashes or left to vultures to devour. I am sure, like me, everyone who attends a funeral falls prey to similar thoughts.

I had tried hard to trace the late Sadhana Bora's life and done a considerable bit of research about it.

Let me start with how she came into our lives. Sometime in late 2013, I got a phone call from a famous lady of Guwahati, the widow of a top cop. She told me that she had picked up an old lady who was found abandoned on the streets. She had given her food and shelter in her house for more than six months. Now with her own advancing age and other commitments, she was finding it hard to look after her. She requested help. Could we accommodate her at Seneh, our home for precisely such destitute old women?

Next morning, two police officers brought a spritely woman, about 65 years of age to Seneh. She was elegantly dressed in a blue-bordered, light pastel sari and a matching blouse. Lightly built, of moderate height, she wore an artificial pearl necklace and matching earrings. Her short hair, dyed black, was neatly parted in the middle. The hair flowed down to cover her ears. Her lips were dabbed with lipstick and her eyebrows elegantly plucked. Her face was powdered generously. Unlike others who were picked up from the streets by our volunteers, this lady looked educated and seemed to be from an aristocratic background.

The police officers told me that the woman had been sent by their ex-boss's widow. The first question that came to my mind was this: how could a woman like the one standing in front of us, be a homeless destitute? The police officers told us that the lady, whose name was Sadhana, had no one in the world after the death of her 23-year-old son, a bachelor. He had been working in a factory as a sales executive and the two of them used to live in rented accommodation. But he died suddenly, two days after contacting encephalitis.

Sadhana had no other means of income or support, no place to stay and hence had become a homeless destitute. In reply to my questions, she would start a diatribe that was ten times more than what normally was required as an answer. I had to forcibly cut her short in between, to ask the next question, or to talk to the officers.

By our criteria, Sadhana qualified to be a resident of Seneh. She was above fifty, had no one to support her, and had no roof or means of sustenance. She fitted the bill completely. She stayed back.

Thereafter, every day, we had to listen to daily complaints from our nurses and housekeepers. The foremost complaint was about her nonstop blabbering.

Next, her abhorrence to any physical work was very marked. To keep the old residents busy and to give them a feeling of a home where they would live like sisters, we had devised a system in which all the essential tasks are carried out by the residents themselves. The healthy and capable are required to cook all the three meals for themselves and the others, by turn, according to a roster. So is the case with sweeping, swabbing, cleaning the toilets and the bath houses.

Sadhana would point-blank refuse to do any such work, even if she was vehemently ticked off. On the other hand, she was fond of ordering others to do these jobs as if she was the employer and they were maids. Invariably, those who listened to her commands were the unfortunate psychiatric patients, who were very submissive because of the psychiatric drugs they were taking. But others would protest and verbal duels would follow. In addition to the household jobs, the residents are expected to learn and practice hobbies like needle work, knitting, weaving, embroidery, pickle making, artificial flower making, and sewing.

Normally, some volunteers with specific knowledge about a particular job come to the premises and teach the residents. Sadhana, however, was always reluctant to participate in such activities.

The fourth complaint was that her hair was infested with lice. She refused to use anti-lice shampoo and was reluctant to get a haircut.

We decided to consult the psychiatrist. He prescribed regular medication. When she was being examined, she kept protesting that she was not mad. So making her swallow the tablets was a big challenge. We devised a surreptitious way of giving her the medicine by crushing the tablets and mixing them with her meals. She, therefore, constantly complained of the food being bitter.

But the ruse worked. It changed Sadhana. She became less talkative and more accommodating. She seems to have quietened down. But her abhorrence to work could not be shaken off. Then suddenly she revealed her real interests: knitting and music. She was an expert in knitting sweaters with intricate patterns. In fact, it can be said she knitted magic. Although her voice was cracking and shaking because of age, she sang some old Assamese and Hindi songs with perfect tunes and rhythms.

The medication made Sadhana sober and genial. Her tendency of ordering others to do her work also waned. She started gelling well with the other inmates. The next battle was to get rid of her lice. Use of the shampoo that claimed to kill lice did not show the desired results. The doctors advised trimming her hair short. But Sadhana would not comply. One day, I showed her a photograph of Marilyn Monroe and told her that she was considered the most beautiful woman in the world in her time. I told her that one of the reasons for her being considered the most beautiful woman, was the way she trimmed her hair. I assured her that if her hair was trimmed, she would undoubtedly be the most beautiful woman in our home.

This worked. She agreed and the trimming job was done successfully. Sadhana looked positively much more attractive with her round face and beautiful eyes. Finally, the war against the lice was won.

Sadhana continued to be elegantly dressed with her face smeared with a generous dose of talcum powder. Her hair was also always dyed black. I was eager to find out how she afforded this. While we were generous in distributing essentials like soaps and detergents to the residents, other make-up items were always in short supply. To the best of our knowledge, the residents did not have any money with them to buy such items.

My curiosity was explained by the in-house caretaker of that time. He said he had come to know that Sadhana has a daughter who lived within the city. Her husband, who was a wealthy man, hated Sadhana. He would not even allow his wife to mention her mother before him, let alone help her. So she had been making arrangements to clandestinely send some things across to Sadhana through a messenger. The goodies included new dresses. We discussed the issue and decided to let it continue. But we confronted Sadhana, who had qualified to be a resident because she had told us that she had no one in the world to look after her. When we produced the hard evidence, she told us that it was true. Her son-in-law had thrice driven her out of his house. At the last instance, she was forced to leave though she had nowhere to go. When she was wandering on the streets, the good old widow had taken her home.

Later, we did speak to her son-in-law. He confirmed Sadhana's story and reiterated that he would never allow her near his home, come what may. He refused to tell us the reason why he hated her so much. He was curt and told us that it was none of our business.

Days rolled by. Sadhana became an integral part of the Seneh family. One day, Sadhana informed us excitedly that her daughter had rung up and informed her that her grand-daughter was getting married. Her daughter also said her husband had agreed to let Sadhana visit for two days on condition that she leaves his house on the morning of the third day after the marriage ceremony. Sadhana wanted our permission to go and attend the ceremony, which we promptly granted. On the appointed day, when she was to be picked up, Sadhana woke up long before the others, and, at seven in the morning, was ready, elegantly dressed and made up for the occasion. She waited the whole day, but no one came to take her. Her daughter rang her up in the evening to inform her she will be picked up the next morning for the ceremony.

Once again, at six in the morning, Sadhana was ready. And once again, she waited for the whole day, but alas, to no avail. We rang up her daughter, but she did not take the call. By 4 pm, Sadhana had begun to cry uncontrollably, with all the other residents trying to console her. We also shed some secret tears.

Later, I was curious to know about Sadhana's past. On my persistent questioning, she said that her husband was an executive of the Fertiliser Corporation of India. She had got married to him when she was seventeen without permission, approval or participation of her parents. They came to know each other when he was living inside their compound in an out-house as one of her parents' tenants.

With two offsprings, their conjugal life was a bed of roses. Later, he was transferred from Assam to the fertiliser factory at Trombay, a Mumbai suburb. The family lived there for more than seven years. Thereafter, he started complaining of severe stomach pain and bloating. He also lost weight and was diagnosed as suffering from stomach cancer. They consulted doctor after doctor and the company management, too, did its best as he was loved and respected by the management. But he did not survive. The world crashed around her.

The couple had been very popular and Sadhana was always the leader in organising cultural events in the Corporation's executive club. Her songs and dances were presented whenever some VIP visited the factory. As proof, she took out some old photographs from her trunk. What she had told us was absolutely true. The photographs said it all. She and her team even had a photograph with late YB Chavan, then chief minister of Maharashtra.

When her husband died, her eldest daughter was already married. The company allowed her to stay in the official quarters for six months. By that time, she had received whatever money her late husband had kept in the employee provident fund scheme with matching contributions and gratuity from the company. The company had no provision for pension. He had no life insurance either. The amount was insufficient to cater for her and her school-going son for long.

With whatever money she had, and together with her 16-year-old son, she shifted to the ancestral home of her husband. But for whatever reason, from the very start, she found that she was not welcome at all. Her in-laws were no more. Her two brothers-in-law lived there with their families. They resented her presence. So, she left after spending a couple of years there, and, started living with her daughter in Guwahati.

Life at her daughter's place was miserable since her son-in-law constantly pestered her to find alternative accommodation. She became the reason for constant friction between the husband and wife.

Luckily, when her son finished his studies, he picked up a job in a plywood factory 50 km from her daughter's house. He rented a place to stay and took his mother along. They were very happy there as her son was very caring.

But fate had other plans for Sadhana. After a brief illness, the boy died suddenly at the age of 26, leaving her lonely and desolate. The roads became her home and alms given by passers-by became her means of sustenance. It was from the streets that she ended up with the old lady who later sent her to us. The good old Samaritan accommodated her for more than six months, but her family started resenting Sadhana's presence and she was forced to look for another option. And that was how she ended up with us.

A year and a half before her demise, Sadhana complained of internal pains on her neck. There was a tiny yet discernible swelling on her neck. The doctor who attended to the residents regularly on a voluntary basis, advised us to take her to the Medical College Hospital. Sadhana was diagnosed with cancer of the thyroid gland.

A biopsy report, however, came negative. Even then, the doctors in the hospital decided to remove her thyroid glands. Sadhana vehemently protested. We tried our best to persuade her, but Sadhana would not relent. Ultimately, once again, we adopted a ruse. We promised her a nice dress of fine silk after the operation and presented her two new night-dresses for use while in the hospital. As an exception, the administration also broke their rules and allowed Sadhana to wear the new night dresses instead of the hospital gown.

The bait worked. Sadhana agreed to undergo the operation. The doctors were impressed by our humanitarian work and gave their full attention to her like a VIP and even paid for some of her medication.

Post the operation, Sadhana came back home. In a month, she had regained her health and also resumed some of her old routine. She even got the maximum applause for a dance that she performed and for her participation in a fashion parade where her sashay down the catwalk like a professional model was very much appreciated. The Governor of a nearby state, our chief guest at the annual function, had specially felicitated her for her performance. At the function, a one-act hilarious drama based on her earlier habit of unstoppable blabbering was also presented, generating peels of laughter from the 200-strong audience.

But from January onward, exactly seven months before her demise, Sadhana became reclusive and morose. She would either sit in the veranda like a dove stuck by a hailstorm or sleep quietly on her bed. She lost interest in food. We were upset as we thought that she was again transitioning back to her old self. I even scolded her for her odd, unexplained behaviour. In retrospect, I am now unable to forgive myself for my outbursts.

Once again, on the advice of another voluntary retired doctor, she was sent back to the hospital. On thorough examination and investigations, the doctors diagnosed that she had stomach cancer. They said that the cancer had spread to a substantial part of her stomach. She was referred to the prestigious Dr B Baruah Cancer Institute.

After some more tests and investigations, the specialist pronounced that Sadhana was beyond medical intervention. Then onward, she required palliative care. After a couple of days, our doctors and the two nurses that we had employed decided they would be able to care for her better at Seneh than at the hospital. The Dr B Baruah Cancer Hospital is a very busy place and in spite of their best efforts and intentions, they were unable to give her individual attention. I was away in America in the interim period. I constantly kept track of her illness and was once able to talk to her over the phone. I tried to give her the moral support to face the disease. She promised that she would fight with all the strength she had in her frail body.

As soon as I was back, I immediately went to meet Sadhana. I sat beside her and fed her a few spoons of *khichri,* a rice and lentil gruel. I noticed Sadhana's eyes brightening, as if her will to fight was enforced with my presence. Over the years, we had developed a good chemistry based on trust and love. Feebly, but resolutely, she pronounced, 'Sir, you are back! Please bless me. Tomorrow, I will stand up again.'

The next day, she did stand momentarily, but immediately thereafter, collapsed on the bed, exhausted and spent.

In the meantime, our office informed her son-in-law about Sadhana's illness. He and his wife came and sat beside her and consoled her. One of our nurses heard him asking her, 'Have they informed Prakash?' (The name used here is fictitious, but the person is real). The nurse informed one of our trustees, who was also present. She cornered the son-in-law and asked him who Prakash was. On her insistence, he revealed that Prakash was Sadhana's eldest son who worked in a fertiliser factory in Namrup, some 300 km from Guwahati. He also disclosed that Sadhana had one more son who was a small-time businessman.

When I heard this, I was livid. Sadhana had cheated us by not disclosing the fact that she had two sons apart from the one who had died. Giving shelter to someone who has living sons is against our rules, and I resented her presence at that point and decided against meeting her again. But we continued our nursing care that was our moral responsibility.

On the third day, as soon as I reached Seneh, our caretaker informed me that I must see Sadhana at once. He said, 'Since yesterday, she has refused even water and is weeping constantly.'

I went and sat on her bed. She summoned all her strength to bend and touch my feet and said, 'Sir, I know I have done an unpardonable deed. I am a sinner. But sir, I am also a mother. How can I tell all of you that I have given birth to two animals and not human beings? Please sir, you can give me whatever punishment you decide. But do not curse them. Please bless them. I want them to be happy. I will bless them even from heaven.' I was stunned, shocked and bewildered, as if lightning had struck me. I was speechless.

It was then that I realised the true nature of motherhood. I said to myself: 'Mothers, you are great, you are the pride of mankind. You are beautiful, you are the ocean of love, you are the hope, you are divine. I salute each mother and bow my head in reverence.'

For four and a half years, Sadhana had hidden in her

heart the pain of her children's ruthless behaviour and neglect of their mother without betraying it even once. She had danced, sung and engaged in merry making as a façade to hide her disappointment and sense of despair. She had never revealed to us, not even once, the pain and fire she was carrying in her heart.

She then narrated to us how her eldest son had never intervened when his wife ruthlessly tortured her and hit her a number of times with blunt firewood when she had stayed with them after her husband's death. She also told us how her other son threw her and her youngest son out from his house (which actually had been built by her husband) and had kept both of them hungry for days. That explained Sadhana's mental maladies that we had at least been able to solve to a large extent.

Her sons must have surely come to know about her health from their brother-in-law. Her daughter also confirmed to us that they had been informed. But none came or even enquired from us about her health. Fifteen days prior to her painful death, she told me, 'Sir, I know they will come. I will bless them. Please be nice to them, but pray do not allow them to take me away from here.' Alas! her last hope also remained unfulfilled.

She conveyed to us another last wish: She wanted to be cremated at the Bhootnath Crematorium where her youngest son had been cremated. We fulfilled her wish.

One day before her death, in delirium, she blurted

out, 'Oh, you both have come. I have made rice pudding for them. Please give it to them.'

This is the sad story of a mother who died a painful death of both body and soul. She was cremated in the same crematorium where her youngest son, who had given her all the love and respect a mother deserves, also rested. Unfortunately, this last vestige of hope and solace for Sadhana Bora was snatched away prematurely by fate, leaving her a mental wreck. With his demise, Sadhana lost the last straw to hang on to, in the cruel ocean of life.

Our two nurses, who had tended to her in a way very few children will do, to their own mothers, performed her last rites. These young girls are the epitome of hope in an otherwise ruthlessly self-centred society of today.

I have intentionally not taken the actual names of her heartless sons, because, I felt, that would have pained Sadhana. The entire story is based on what she narrated to me and on a few circumstantial evidences. For example, every 31 January, Sadhana would pester us to take her to the crematorium to light a candle for her dead son. I have not done any research to know more about her past. The question that repeatedly haunts me is. Even if Sadhana was a difficult person to deal with, or, she had done things in the past that embarrassed and alienated her sons, did these absolve them of the sin of not once coming to see her, when she was in the jaws of death? Neither did they attend her funeral.

They lacked human feelings and respect for their mother from whose womb they had seen the first light of life. They failed to show even the slightest of respect and gratitude that a mother deserves. Wherever they are, I pray to God that he gives them happiness and peace of mind and, when they are old, I wish their own children love, respect and care for them.

Author's note: This is the translation of an article I wrote for a local newspaper some time back. After it was published, among the many calls of appreciation that came, one in particular was significant. This gentleman told me he knew Sadhana's eldest son and that he had never hated a man as much as he did after he read the story. He was more than sure that the son had read the piece too, since he was not seen in public for a good many days after that. I told him it was never my intention to belittle her family. My intention, instead, was to raise a toast to motherhood.

Manju Bhattacharya

Her Environment Made Her Who She Is

'My mother died when I was seven,' narrated Manju in her sleepy, hoarse, husky and somewhat intimidating voice. 'Whenever I close my eyes, I remember her pretty face. She was a very petite woman, who would tell me stories till late at night and keep me in her arms in the hard bed we had, till I fell asleep.'

Her mother was, indeed, a beautiful woman: tall, well proportioned, suave and elegant. From Manju's countenance and physical attributes, one could easily make out her pedigree. She was certainly from a well-off family. Her mother was married to a handsome man, a high official in the Assam Secretariat at Shillong, the erstwhile capital of undivided Assam. Her husband died young, leaving her in the care of his family. They had no children.

What made the family abandon Manju's mother in a state-run home for destitute women first at Shillong, later in Nagaon, Assam after just two years of widowhood, and that too with an unborn child in her womb, is difficult to imagine. Was she a victim of abuse by a man who was a part of the family after her husband's death? Did that lead to her banishment to save the family's honour? This, anyway, was suggested by someone who worked in the state-run home where Manju was born.

Manju says her mother used to tell her about a very wicked uncle whom Manju should ignore if he ever came calling. We would not like to hazard a guess about who sired Manju. The truth is that Manju was born in a destitute home, and her father's name kept blank in the register. Her mother, who remained aloof and withdrawn, brought her up till she was seven in the same home for destitute women.

The mother then died of unknown reasons. One source said she committed suicide. Manju vehemently disagrees. Unfortunately, the caretaker of the Nagaon home is in her late eighties now, and her memory is not very coherent. Her daughter, who had given us some details, is thirty years younger to Manju. Whatever information she offered was from her mother's accounts and they are scanty. We could not find a verifiable source to map Manju's childhood days. I have pieced together titbits of information I gathered from various sources.

Manju's ordeal in life, her lonely struggle to grow up, keep alive and fight against unparalleled and insurmountable odds, began with the death of her mother. She was shifted to an orphanage after her mother passed away.

Young Manju then came under the care of paid social workers. Some of the employees of the state-run orphanage were kind and considerate, but some were harsh and ruthless, who would physically punish the orphans at the slightest provocation.

Young Manju was a beautiful, smart and fun-loving girl of a somewhat rebellious nature. To top it all, she was a bundle of energy, possessed an elephantine memory and had a knack for mischief. Generally, the social workers were very fond of her. However, for a few others, she was a source of trouble and hence often faced their ire.

In the orphanage, food was scarce, clothes were few and the source of entertainment for the children limited. The children were sent to an elementary school that had only one teacher, an old lady. Fortunately, I was able to talk to an old lady (now deceased) who used to frequent the school in those days. According to her, Manju was the brightest of the thirty-odd girls who attended the primary school. Hence, she had organised Manju's post-primary education in a Bengali medium high school outside the orphanage. Manju studied there till Class X, then appeared for her matriculation examination and failed. This ended her academic pursuits. Manju says she had the unique distinction of being the only child from the orphanage who studied till tenth grade. Even today, she is very proud of it.

At an early age, Manju developed the habit of stealing small things from all and sundry and without pretensions, confided in me that she had earned the sobriquet, Suruni, an Assamese word for female thief. Unfortunately, later, we discovered it was a psychological condition on which she had no control, and she never got cured of it. We will speak about it when we discuss her present-day persona later in the story.

She grew up to be an attractive, lithe young woman, supple and graceful with a lot of energy and an intellect which unfortunately could not flourish because of lack of opportunity and the right environment. Even today, at seventy-plus, she sometimes surprises us, by dashing off a poem at the drop of a hat. The poems normally have substance and rhythm, although they require a bit of pruning and nurturing here and there. However, the kind of life she led and the environment she grew up in, robbed her of suppleness and coherence in her thought process.

From what she told me and from the information I gathered from different sources, and from the matron of the orphanage where Manju lived, she was transferred to another home for grown-ups at Guwahati when she was sixteen. This was the environment that developed the personality traits that have since stayed with her. This home had young and middle-aged women from varied backgrounds, some rescued from brothels by the police, others abandoned by their husbands and society for unknown reasons, as well as a few who suffered from various forms of mental health issues. There were also girls like Manju, who came from orphanages. Manju, therefore, picked up quite a few good as well as bad habits from her compatriots.

We noticed several contradictions in Manju's character from the day she came to us. Sometimes, she surprised us all with her recitation of a few Sanskrit verses, which she was also able to translate. When angry or provoked by fellow residents, she could erupt like a volcano and could shoot out a volley of crude and explicitly vulgar obscenities at her hapless target. In the prayer hall, she could become an epitome of tranquillity and devotion. When complaining about someone, she could cry like a child, as if she had a hidden reservoir of tears that could flow unchecked once the floodgates were opened. Yet again, when caught stealing, she could put on such an innocent face that one instantly felt pity for her.

At the government-run destitute home, the authorities managed to engage Manju as an Anganwadi worker, whose duty involved travelling from house to house to motivate rural women to earn independently to augment the family income. However, she was fired after two years. I suspect, it was her fickle and fastidious nature that must have come in her way. Back in the home where she had stayed earlier, her frustration and feeling of neglect and apathy made her a rebel. She would pick up a fight on frivolous issues and wilfully defy orders. She stayed there till she was fifty-five, when she was transferred to yet another government-run home for older women.

Her real ordeal started there. The home was in an isolated area. The campus was huge, with only a few women inhabitants. The atmosphere, according to a social activist who used to frequent the home, was hostile, the manager being somewhat of a misogynist. At times, she was positively ruthless.

The rebel in Manju could never accept this new change quietly. She felt her freedom, or, what she conceived as her right, were being transgressed upon. She protested vocally with words that were unkind and harsh. It provoked all, especially the workers running the Home. To top it all, her uncontrollable urge to steal anything including the most useless articles and her wandering habit (she could be missing for hours, walking aimlessly in the adjoining jungles without anyone's knowledge, causing panic in the establishment) provoked the caretakers to be extremely harsh with her.

They would tie her up in a room and beat her mercilessly.

This, I must admit, was the unofficial account that I heard from the social worker, who also happened to be the daughter of the elderly matron of the orphanage. I also heard Manju's own version of her story. There was proof in the tell-tale marks of beatings on her body when she was brought to Seneh. The faded marks can be seen even today, after more than seven years.

Like all other residents of our home, except a few, there is no proof of age available, so we can only guess at Manju's age. We estimate it to be around sixty-five on her arrival at Seneh.

Rescuing her was an ordeal in itself. The first hurdle was the State's Social Welfare Department. We had to make many a trip to the District and State Welfare Offices to get her released. Ultimately, we had to go to court and give an undertaking under oath that we would take care of her for the rest of her life. The entire process took almost four months.

When Manju came in, she was a mere skeleton of a woman: bruised, physically weak, and hardly able to walk around, but mentally alert and sharp. Within days of her arrival, we realised that she abhorred discipline. According to the rules, all the residents are required to bathe and get dressed by eight in the morning, for prayers. Manju would invariably get up late and straightaway proceed to the kitchen to make a cup of tea. If prevented, she would throw tantrums and use explicitly vulgar language to curse the caretakers. Quite often, she would be found missing, having either gone for a walk on the streets or to the nearest shop to try to shoplift something or the other. The gates had to be locked to prevent this. She would also pick up fights with other inmates at the slightest provocation. She could sometimes get physical. But as mentioned before, she could also howl like a child.

The biggest challenge for all of us was her habit of stealing. It could be anything a blouse, a powder puff, some rice, sugar or cooked items from the kitchen. There was no discernible pattern. Her bed sometimes stank of stale food, because she would hide the loot under her pillow or beneath her bed. Once I called the old residents in batches to my house to interview them to learn more about their past. It was then that Manju told me about being called Suruni.

At our home, we served them all a wholesome lunch. And lo and behold! after the batch that had included Manju left us post-lunch, my wife complained that one of the stainless steel small bowls had gone missing. Later, it was found under Manju's bed.

I could relate to Manju's psychological condition because in my youth when I had lived as a bachelor in an Air Force Mess, I had come across a senior officer, a doctor by profession, who was a known kleptomaniac. He used to live alone in the mess since his family was away.

Once, two of us, young subalterns, had climbed up a drainpipe and jumped up to his balcony in his absence, to get hold of some medicine for a toothache for a colleague's wife. And we found to our amusement, stolen stuff kept under his bed or the mattress. The items included sanitary towels (positively he had no use for them) and myriads of medicines, syringes and other medical items picked up from the hospital where he was the chief. We lifted a half-litre bottle of clove oil from his room, and hence became the proud healers of toothaches of the ladies of the station!

That was when I had first learnt about the psychological condition called kleptomania. So, I instantly understood the reasons for Manju's behaviour and had full sympathy for her. But it was very difficult to convince the others, her co-inhabitants and the caretakers alike. We tried to explain to them that it was a psychological condition, over which Manju had no control. Unfortunately, this did not cut much ice with the others, and so complaints pour in even today. I have narrated a small incident involving Manju in Bina's story earlier.

With proper nutrition and dietary supplements, Manju's health improved fast. Now, with renewed energy, Manju threw new challenges for the caretakers. That is when we decided that she needed to be kept busy. We asked her what she could do. She told us she could knit. And what an artisan she is. The first thing she knitted was a scarf for me, which I always use in winter. She knits relentlessly, churning out quality wear. Visitors book her woollens before they are completed.

Once, Manju came to me and handed me a poem in Assamese. I was astonished at her imagination and creativity. After a little editing and refining, the poem was published in a popular weekly and in a yearly magazine. It is beyond my comprehension where and how Manju acquired such talent in her turbulent life.

Manju today is a picture of tranquillity and serenity. Astonishingly, it is quite some time now since we have received any complaint of theft. She keeps to herself and keeps knitting the whole day. The grin on her face tells it all.

Unfortunately, her health is deteriorating. She is gradually becoming weak and quiet. The doctors attribute it to old age and to malnutrition in her growing years. She hardly ever ventures out. The need to keep the gates closed to prevent her from wandering out has become rare. Her indomitable spirit, however, eggs her on to be the first to volunteer for a new programme in the home, although we try to dissuade her. What a wonderful spirit this woman of substance has and her physical weaknesses and ill-health will never be able to sap her spirit.

Author's Note: A day before the book was sent to print, Manju breathed her last after prolonged sickness. Her last few words were all praise and blessings to the Seneh family.

Sarala Kalita

Beating All Odds

Gaurikanta Kalita jumped in joy when he heard the birth cry of a newborn from the locked room where a midwife was helping his wife deliver their first child. After a while, when the midwife came out to announce the birth of a baby girl, his joy knew no bounds. The baby was born after four years of conjugal life. The long wait had given them the jitters.

Gaurikanta had secretly made a promise that he would offer a special puja to Ma Kamakhya, a temple of Lord Shiva's consort Parvati situated on top of the Kamakhya hills near Guwahati. Hindus believe the temple is one of the seven most sacred places of pilgrimage. Having a girl as the first child is considered a good omen in the North East.

On the night of the sixth day after birth, according to their customs, a pen made of an eagle feather, a blank white paper, a bottle of ink, and a lighted earthen mustard oil-fuelled *saki* (an oil lamp with a cotton wick) was placed on a table by the infant's bed. It was believed that Bidhata, the God who decides the fortunes of every human being, visits a newborn on the sixth night and writes her future on the sheet of blank paper. Needless to say, the next morning, the paper would remain blank. But then, how can normal human beings read what God has written? Won't it be blasphemous to ask God or even try to know what he had surreptitiously written in the middle of the night?

Social customs and beliefs kept the infant confined to her room till the eleventh day, when in the morning, the other ladies of the household laid a *pira* (a low broad wooden stool) covered with a fresh banana leaf. On this, a lighted *saki*, a piece of oval-shaped stone normally used for grinding, and a bowl of water were kept with some flowers. A small fire was lit by burning hay on the ground by the side of the *pira*. The baby was then placed on the *pira* by the mother, supporting the baby with both hands. The eldest among the attending ladies, then, directed the mother to lift the child and hold her momentarily first over the fire, simultaneously chanting 'Do not die of fire', then over the water, to the chant 'Do not die of drowning' and last over the stone, chanting 'Do not die of any hard or sharp object'. Thereafter, the infant was placed on the *pira* again, supported by another lady. Then the mother bowed on all fours to the Sun God, requesting that He light up the baby's tomorrows. The ceremony ended with the attending ladies sounding the *Uruli*, a musical sound made by rotating the tongue tip on the lips and blowing strongly to produce a ringing, vibratory sound.

With the passing days, the baby grew wonderfully well, plump and attractive. They named her Sarala, meaning simpleton. By the time she was three months old, the mother started having a nagging doubt. She felt the baby was unable to make eye contact with her as was expected at that age. However, she kept her doubts to herself, and tried experimenting quietly to prove this wrong. She would stealthily bring a light to the dark room but the baby did not seem to notice it. She also saw white spots on the pupils.

One morning, after her husband returned from the fields, washed and then went to lift up to cuddle the baby girl, the frightened mother confided her lurking fears to him. They consulted some of the elders, who told them that some babies took longer to fix their eyes on an object. The couple waited till the baby was six months old. But alas, even after six months, the baby was unable to make eye contact. Her other sensory attributes, on the other hand, seemed to be developing faster than normal.

Finally, they took the baby to a nearby doctor, who confirmed their worst fears. The baby was visually impaired. He suggested the baby be taken to an ophthalmologist. The ophthalmologist pronounced that the baby had an incurable eye condition and would be deprived of sight all her life. The couple felt as if the sky had fallen on their heads. Clasping the baby to her bosom, the young mother cried for days.

Gaurikanta lived in a village about 100 km from Guwahati. He was a hardworking simpleton. His family had a sizeable piece of ancestral land that produced enough rice and mustard for their livelihood. They were an undivided family, he and three of his cousins living together. Gaurikanta had no blood brother. They lived side by side in thatched huts and did the farm work together, dividing the responsibilities equally, with the womenfolk helping them in the planting and harvesting of the ripe paddy and mustard.

Gauri was the healthiest and the most hardworking. He ungrudgingly put in more efforts in the farming process. The entire land holding was still in their grandfather's name. The land was fertile and unlike the low-lying areas nearby, their land was never inundated in the seasonal floods that ravaged most of the countryside. In addition to the farm land, they had also inherited a large compound around the houses. It was dotted with fruit-bearing trees and a bamboo grove in one corner.

That's not all. A huge area was also available for their kitchen garden. A sizeable pond doubled as a source of water for the family and also as a fishery. A mechanical hand pump provided drinking water The large joint family had enough to eat and live comfortably. Unfortunately, relations between the cousins gradually soured over the years because of some small misunderstandings involving the children.

By the time Sarala was three, she had a brother and a second one was on its way. She mastered the art of moving around unassisted in the familiar areas of the compound. At times, though, she would run after the other toddlers and crash into a wall or a tree. Her wails would bring her mother racing towards her.

With her hair combed into two long plaits hanging down on either side of her face, dressed in a white dress dotted with black polka, Sarala undoubtedly was the most attractive girl child, not only in the household, but in the entire neighbourhood. She had another advantage over her peers. She would always be the first to hear the sound of a falling ripe mango, guava or a peach and rush to the spot much before the others. That invariably caused squabbles between the children. At times, even the mothers got involved.

Apart from that, Sarala got more attention and love from her neighbours, probably out of pity, but this made the other women of the joint family envious. Sometimes, it resulted in verbal duels between them. Sarala's over-protective mother got singled out. The squabbles, however, later turned into fights between her father and his cousins. Matters reached a head when Gaurikanta came to know that his cousins had, by fraudulent means, usurped all the fertile land and registered it in their names, leaving just a small infertile piece for him. It devastated him and broke the heart of the simple, honest man.

He sold off the piece of land in his name, left his ancestral village, lock, stock and barrel and proceeded with his family to a remote and somewhat secluded place far away, where an acquaintance had migrated earlier. There he bought some land and also managed to occupy half an acre of government land. He constructed a simple thatch-roofed, bamboo house and started life anew. By that time, his third son was born.

Three years later, he had established himself comfortably in his new abode. The family was happy. Their neighbours were friendly and helpful.

Young Sarala was a happy child. She moved around in familiar places unassisted, mimicked the birds, sang a line or two from popular Assamese songs and started learning the alphabet on her own, by listening to the others who read aloud. Her parents, and even some neighbours, were astounded by her memory, intellect and astuteness. She would remember a part of a song along with its tune if she heard it once. She could tell what an object was simply by touching and feeling it once.

She also remembered whatever words the grown-ups uttered and repeated them correctly. Her sense of smell was phenomenal. From a considerable distance, she could tell what her mother was cooking, what flower was blooming or even if rain was on its way to where they lived.

The parents decided to send her to a residential blind school located 300 km from their home. It was the most famous school in Assam for the visually impaired. When her father left her there, she cried uncontrollably and clung to him. The warden had to forcibly take her away. Thus started a new life for the six-year-old.

In just six months, young Sarala got used to her new routine. By seven, she proved herself as one of the brightest girls in school. She adapted to the Braille system of learning and learnt to read and write. In the fifth grade, she came first in class, which continued till she finished high school. Along with her studies, she also started learning vocal music. Within a year, she also developed the skill to play the harmonium and sing along with it.

'We had a wonderful time at school. The teachers were dedicated and kind except for one whom we had nicknamed the "devil". The dormitories were spacious, the food reasonably good; hostel life was full of fun. I made quite a few friends there. After I finished school, for about three years, I kept in touch with four of my classmates and hostel friends. Unfortunately, I have lost contact with all now,' said Sarala, describing that phase of her life.

When eighteen, Sarala completed her matriculation with flying colours, securing a first division with distinction in mathematics. Simultaneously, guided by her kind school's music teacher, she also completed her *Visarad* (graduation) in music from the famous Bhatkhande Institute of Music. She was a student of the distant learning curriculum of the Institute.

Schooling over, she went back home. Her two brothers, now sixteen and fourteen, had grown up to be healthy youths. Both would trek 3-km to school. With five people to feed, as well as cater to the education of his two sons, Gaurikanta, who by that time, did not enjoy good health, found it difficult to make ends meet. To add to his miseries, his two sons were not keen on farming. Sarala, too, abhorred physical work. Nevertheless, Gaurikanta admitted Sarala, because of her academic record to a local college. But there was no Braille-trained teacher, and Sarala was unable to cope with her studies.

Khowang Bayang hailed from Arunachal, the eastern-most province of India, a hilly area on the great Himalayan ranges, sharing a common border with Tibet. Different tribes with their own distinct culture, dialect and dressing habits inhabit the state. The twenty-one-year-old Khowang had come to visit his aunt who was married in a village not far from Sarala's village. His cousin sister was a classmate of Sarala's.

At nineteen, Sarala was a beautiful woman, tall, lean, fair, with perfect cheek bones, lustrous long black hair, and a captivating smile that never left her lips. Her taut skin was smooth and unblemished. Khowang was instantly attracted to her. Her visual impairment was of no consequence for him. He went back to his native village and started writing long letters to her.

Their love blossomed like a rose bud, full of fresh fragrance. He proposed, she accepted, and her parents heaved a sigh of relief. They were married in a simple ceremony. He took her to the hills where her in-laws lived. Adjusting to the new, hilly terrain was a challenge, but her superb instinct and extraordinary sensory powers made it possible for her to adjust. She also started enjoying the cool air, imagining that the gentle breeze that fanned her face was like the gentle caresses of her mother when she was a young child.

The soothing smell of the flowering trees of the nearby jungles in summer and the pine cones intoxicated her. She would sing aloud, when alone, in pure joy and ecstasy.

Although their food habits were different, she adjusted to the new cuisine like a fish in a household aquarium, within its limited surroundings. Gradually, she started helping her mother-in-law in cooking. She said to me, 'I was able to do the cooking in the kitchen alone in a few months. I knew exactly where the spices were kept and by feeling with my hands, I could select the spice I wanted, or the salt.'

Meanwhile, Khowang found a job as an office boy in a government office around 50 km away. Initially, he lived alone in government quarters. Six-odd months thereafter, she too moved to the place where he worked. There she conceived. When she announced the heart-warming tidings to Khowang, he was overjoyed and hugged her tenderly, as if she was a baby. The next day, he distributed sweets in his office. But alas, before the full term was up, she aborted a dead foetus. The duo was devastated.

The normally ebullient Sarala became silent like a lamb, only responding in monosyllables to his questions in a somewhat guttural voice. Even today, when singing a song soothingly, suddenly such a voice emanates from her throat, spoiling the effect and melody of the song.

Her depressed mood worried Khowang. He became restless. When some of his friends offered him a glass of locally brewed *madhu*, a hard and strong country liquor, he had it without protest. Gradually, it turned into a habit. He found it lightened his mind and soothed his frayed nerves. Sarala protested initially, but with the passage of time, she got used to the heady smell he carried with him when he returned home after a few drinks.

And, then, she conceived again and the sad saga of a second abortion was repeated, once again disrupting their lives and shattering their dreams. What she expected from her husband now was a warm shoulder to cry on and a comforting hug. But, instead, he openly showed his disdain for her and turned into an absolute alcoholic. Their relationship became tumultuous and, at times, violent. His drinking bouts increased. She also learnt that he was seeing another woman whom he wanted to bring home as his second wife. It was common to have more than one wife in their society. (I once met a diminutive man, an official in the Arunachal government, who boasted of having nine wives. I am told this scourge has almost disappeared with education, increased contact with the outside world and strict government vigil.)

Khowang finally brought home his second wife.

Frustrated, disillusioned and devastated, Sarala decided to leave him forever. With the help of a common friend, she came back home and knocked on the doors of her parental home. The parents had known about her ordeals and had feared that something like this would happen. With a heavy heart, they welcomed her back. Her father, then sixty, was struggling to earn a living. Old age had caught him unawares. His capacity for hard work had sapped. The two boys were not of much help as they were both lazy and abhorred physical work. So, he had to give out his land on a yearly lease. With his share of the produce reducing to half, sustenance was tough. His eldest son failed his school examinations and left for Guwahati to find his own way, learnt driving and became a truck driver.

Sickness associated with old age, hardships and his daughter's turbulent life, finally compelled Gaurikanta to sell his property, pack his bags and shift to Guwahati, a terrible city to live in, if one is poor. Its anatomy is difficult to explain, its arteries branching out like roots of a tree in random patterns, some arteries so constricted that the city's lifeblood passes through them with real difficulty.

Sadly, the city has no functioning heart or lungs. Land sharks, without any regulation or planning by the authorities, thoughtlessly developed parts of it. This destroyed the ecology, beauty, grandeur and the vitality of the lustrous green hills that dot the landscape in and around the city.

Gaurikanta finally bought a piece of land cheap because the land actually belonged to the state, but had been forcefully occupied by a land shark by bribing politicians as well as officials. It was a small piece, barely enough to construct a house of three small rooms and an adjoining kitchen. His house had a cast iron roof, wooden poles and bamboo walls plastered with a lightly coated cement and sand mix. The largest of the rooms went to the family of the eldest son who had shared the cost of construction and had two children.

Of the three remaining rooms, the smallest doubled as a living room and the younger son's bedroom. Later, the younger son, a high school dropout, also left home to work as the helper of a truck driver in a nearby town. In a few years, he had graduated to driving trucks. He came home occasionally and helped them financially. After a couple of years, he brought home a wife, who turned out to be very quarrelsome. One fine morning, the couple left and never returned.

Time went by and eventually, Gaurikanta exhausted all his savings. The son did not earn enough to feed them all. Life became tough for the family. To top it all, Sarala, with her disability and somewhat irritating behaviour, soon became a cause of discord in the family. The daughter-in-law did not get along with Sarala.

The struggle for survival was real. The son and his wife prioritised provision of food to the family members in the following order first, the two children, next themselves, then the old parents, and last, Sarala.

According to Sarala, her sister-in-law always belittled her, making fun of her disability, and kept suggesting that she go out and sit in the nearest street corner and beg. 'How could she suggest this to me, a first division Higher Secondary pass woman and accomplished singer? Could I take up such a demeaning profession? If I had the money to pay a bribe, I could have been a Social

Welfare official, like a few other lucky ones with similar difficulties,' lamented Sarala.

Her story about the few other lucky ones turned out to be true. Unfortunately, such stories abound in India, where corruption has eaten away the values and virtues of our country, and continues to ruin progress and development. The poor are the main victims.

We heard from one of their neighbours about the sad plight of a blind woman living with her old parents in his neighbourhood. He told us that unless someone turned up to help her, she would be forced to beg, and also with her attractive, youthful looks, she might even be exploited physically. In May 2012, I went with a colleague to meet Sarala. The mud path was sloppy, slimy and slippery because of the monsoon in its full fury. We finally entered the living room with its two rickety plastic chairs and a bed with a tattered sheet and mattress.

An old man emerged with sunken eyes, dishevelled unkempt hair, and an unruly, roughly trimmed beard, looking positively undernourished and sick. When we explained the reason for our visit, he sobbed like a child whose mother had slapped him for unruly behaviour. Then his wife came out, a skeleton of a woman loosely draped in a torn Mekhela Chadar.

After learning why we were there, she went in and brought out Sarala, who was wearing a cheap black pair of sunglasses and was dressed in a dirty, torn, and stained kurta-pyjama. She was thin like a straw, her cheekbones jutting out prominently, definitely a proof of malnourishment. Her facial skin was furrowed and her hands were shaking nervously. She narrated her tale of woe. Her brother gave food barely enough for one. So they had devised a method of sharing the meal. Each one would have a full meal and wait for a day and half for the next.

We summoned her sister-in-law and she narrated the extent of the poverty they were going through. Our offer of taking Sarala to our facilities and our promise to look after her for the rest of her life was welcomed with enthusiasm. The old man embarrassed me by falling at my feet, asking me to promise that we would look after their unfortunate daughter and treat her well. We assured him and volunteered to take him along with her so that he could have a look at the facilities at Seneh and return satisfied.

Sarala was brought in the next day and admitted to the Seneh family. We have provided her with a harmonium and she is always busy in the morning hours practising music. If you ask Sarala about her visual impairment, she has a stock story to tell. First, she says that she could see till she was three. One day, she sustained injuries to her eyes. Some local herbal medications applied to the eyes culminated in her blindness.

Probably, the poor lady had forgotten what she told

us because when I asked her to repeat her story, another time, she told me a different one. This time, she said that when she was four, she woke up one morning with her eyes swollen and closed with thick mucus. Her parents applied herbal medication on her eyes. It resulted in her loss of vision permanently. We did consult two separate ophthalmologists and both of them opined that she had been blind from birth.

I have no explanation about her astonishing sense of colour. If you ask her to select the yellow dress from among a pile of clothes, she will fetch it accurately. And this even when the stack of dresses is exactly of the same material. Another day, I led her to a flowering tree, and made her touch a blooming flower and asked her to identify its colour. She could do it accurately.

She is, however, a very lazy person who abhors physical work even work that a sightless person can easily do. If we insist, she flaunts her disability and cries like a child to curry special favours.

She sings well and often astonishes us with her clean knitting abilities. I often wear her hand-knitted sweaters when I visit Seneh. A light touch and she is able to recognise it and boasts about it.

She is around sixty now, and is on regular medication for high blood pressure and diabetes. She appears positively happy and content. What is most gratifying for us is when we see Sukhi, who despite her psychological issues and the fact that she can hardly hear or speak legibly, holding Sarala's hand and leading her around. What a motivating pair they make!

Taarani Basumatary

A Fairytale Life That Went Awry

New buds had sprouted from the freshly planted cuttings from old plants. She knew that by next week, six to nine such stalks would deliver fresh green leaves standing erect and strong. The land that lay before her eyes till the furthest point where the sky touched the earth in her field of vision, would soon turn into a green bed of dancing long leaves, giving life to the otherwise barren, brown expanse. She loved the smell of the young, curvaceous leaves of the sugarcane fields of her village. The leaves merrily danced with the breeze heroically withstanding even the lashing rains. She loved to touch the tip of the leaves with her palms.

Their village was exquisitely beautiful. It was dotted with a few yellow flowering Sonaru (*Cassia Fistula*) trees, three or four Modar (*Erythrina Indica*) trees that would emblazon the sky with its big reddish flowers in season, and, a majestic large gregarious Hollong (*Diptero Carpus Macro Carpus*) that stood like a colossus in the middle of the village, as if keeping a watchful vigil on it. All but one of the houses of their village were constructed of bamboo frames with a thatched roof. The walls of flattened bamboos were plastered with a thick mixture of earth and cow dung. The earthen floors were similarly plastered with a thin mix of earth and dung that kept it both smooth and dust-free. Each house had a large compound separated from the other by delicately woven bamboo fencing. Invariably, the large courtyard in front of the houses had three or four flowering trees, including hibiscus, and the night flowering jasmine. A few shrubs of Nayantara here and there yielded colourful small flowers round the year. Each house had a small pond at its rear that provided water for the household as well as a mini fishery. In each boundary, small or big, the two sides had a perfect line of tall thin beetle nut trees. Every house had a bamboo grove at the rear end touching the boundary fencing, and an open sunny area for growing seasonal vegetables.

There was a lonely path by the side of the Hollong tree. It led to a few houses in one corner of the village.

It was rumoured that the tall 'Burra Dangoria' (a fabled ghost attired in white from turban to toe) lived inside the hollow trunk of the tree. On dark nights, he emerged from his abode and stood tall and elegant, looking out with his big round eyes that glittered like stars.

There were stories galore of pedestrians passing through, especially in the dark phase of the moon, and seeing the Burra Dangoria standing atop the small hillock where the tree stood, his eyes shining like those of a tiger out on a night prowl.

It was intriguing that the ghost appeared only when someone passed by alone. Sometimes, at night, one could see a small fire atop the marshy area in front of the tree. It was rumoured that the fire was lit by the Burra Dangoria to roast young children whom he caught at night. In living history, though, no child ever went missing from the village. However, that did not do much to discredit the roasting theory. When one of the villagers, a student of a college in the nearby town, tried to explain the phenomenon as a will-o'-the-wisp, he had no takers.

Doubts, if any, about the existence of Burra Dangoria completely got obliterated from her young mind when her uncle, a priest, narrated a story of how the Burra Dangoria once stood in his path when he was returning from a late-night *puja* in the village headman's house. The seven feet tall Burra Dangoria was in whites. Without panicking, the priest stood his ground and started chanting the Gayatri Mantra that Hindus believe is a powerful instrument of faith. Burra Dangoria not only refrained from causing any harm, but also bowed to the priest to let him pass.

Tarini, the protagonist of this story, says that she too once confronted the Burra Dangoria in person. It was a winter evening. The sun had not shown its face throughout the day. The atmosphere was damp and dreary and dark clouds hung overhead. There was an eerie feeling in the air. To top it all, her school delayed the students' departure due to a visit by the Inspector of Schools. Dusk had already set in when the eleven-year-old was walking back the three miles to her home. As she crossed the infamous path where the Burra Dangoria was normally spotted, her heart pounded like that of a *dheki,* a device for pounding. It is made out of a long log with a fulcrum in the middle and a heavy pounding rod made out of rounded hard wood, which is used for grinding cereals in rural households in Assam.

She held her books to her chest with her right hand, and with the other, lifted her *mekhela*, an ankle-length skirt worn by the women and girls of the area, and started running with her alert and apprehensive eyes fixed on the tree. And then, in the dusk, she saw him tall and white, standing on his two legs on the mound, leaning against the tree. She could not remember how she reached home. Or what happened thereafter. What she remembered was the worried faces of her mother and brothers, intently gazing at her, when she opened her eyes. Her face was wet with the water they had sprinkled on her face and head. They told her that no sooner had she set foot on the front yard of her house, she shrieked like a wounded canine and fell unconscious.

She narrated what she saw. A neighbour who walked along the path she took, later said that he saw the white bull of one of the villagers nibbling at the tender leaves that sprouted from the lower part of the tree trunk. The bull had propped himself up on his fore legs, his hind legs firmly on the ground.

'I did not believe him. He invented the story to pacify my nerves,' said Tarini. From that day on, she always took the additional mile-long circuitous route to school to avoid the tree.

Tarini's family was very poor. With nine mouths to feed she had six siblings and parents, her father found it hard to manage from his small business of trading vegetables bought from farmers of his village and a few nearby ones. He would then cart them on his bicycle to sell in the small town of Dergaon, 4-km down the road.

He was a Brahmin by caste and was occasionally engaged by a local priest to help him organise rituals in the households where the priest was invited to perform. The family rejoiced when such opportunities came by. As remuneration, he not only earned some money and a dress, but also received a bowl of rice, some lentils, a bottle of cooking oil and a few select vegetables. For two days, they would have sumptuous meals. But such summons were few and far between.

On other days, their meals were frugal. Normally it was rice and a vegetable curry made from whatever remained unsold from her father's business. Occasionally, they would make a curry of small fish caught from their pond. They were also used to sleeping on an empty stomach. One of her siblings, the youngest brother, died early because of malnutrition and lack of proper medication.

'I distinctly remember the day when my mother was humiliated by one of our relatively well-to-do neighbours, who was also a distant relative. Unable to withstand the cries brought upon by the hunger pangs of my five-year-old brother, my mother took him to their house begging for some food. She was driven out as if she were a pariah dog. She came back sobbing and out of sheer desperation, started beating the child. My mother never forgot this humiliation till death. That was a miserable time,' said Tarini to me, recalling this unhappy episode in her childhood that left a scar on her mind.

Earlier, their situation was never that bad. Tarini remembers that her father had a job in a distant town and they lived well. But he left his job to fight a court case against his estranged brothers for property. By the time the case got settled, he was broke.

From her childhood, Tarini developed a very resolute and focussed mind. If she set her eyes on something and fixed a goal, she would leave no stone unturned to achieve it. She had decided that she would pursue her studies, come what may. Her other siblings had dropped out of school and had started working as labourers, because her parents could not support their schooling. But Tarini braved all odds. She walked three miles one way every day in the sweltering heat in summer and in the numbing chill in winter without proper nourishment.

At eighteen, she completed her matriculation with flying colours, the first one in the family to do so. She picked up a job as a *Gram Sevika,* employed by the state to motivate villagers, especially women, to pursue studies and learn methods of self-employment. Whatever she earned, half of it went to her parents towards family expenses. With the other half, she paid her share of the rent for the dormitory accommodation with seven others. Her first posting was at Hatibor, in Nagaon district of Assam. She worked there for two years. The state then sent her to Shantiniketan, the University founded by the Nobel laureate and social reformer, Rabindranath Tagore, for vocational studies.

At twenty-three, she fell in love. It was true love at first sight. He was a simpleton, always neatly attired, soft-spoken with a drooling voice, shy and timid, but firm in principles. The bicycle in which he moved around was always spotlessly clean and well-oiled. His name was Devendra Basumotary. He worked in the same department and was required to visit her workplace on official duties. His bright and slanting eyes, the pupils green in colour, the flat but firm nose, the smooth and taut skin and a mouth with thin but pronounced lips gave him an aura of sensuality that attracted Tarini instantly. When she got the opportunity to talk to him, she was mesmerised with his soft and melodious voice, polite and gentle demeanour tempered with just the right amount of authority and persuasiveness.

Tarini had finally met the man she had been looking for.

Their courtship was intense, sincere and dignified. They met every week. She would sit pillion on his bicycle, and they would go to a secluded place and spend time together, talking. A year later, they decided to marry. There were hurdles to cross, mostly the difference in social and family backgrounds. He was a Boro, an ethnic plains tribesman from a community that has a rich culture and strong social mores. They spoke a dialect different from Assamese, the latter being the common link language of different ethnic groups who inhabit the state. The Boros are a very proud people with strong bonding, who marry within the tribe. It was with extreme caution and apprehension that Devendra took her to his house one Sunday morning for his mother's blessings.

'My heart beat like a drum. I was prepared for rebuff and humiliation, but what I experienced was the most wonderful moments of my life. She looked at me intently for a moment. I was dark-skinned and they were comparatively fairer. I was ready for rejection but she suddenly embraced me and planted a kiss on my cheek, welcoming me as if I was an honoured guest. I instantly knew I was accepted and that I had one more mother to bank on in the future,' she said.

But the euphoric feeling vanished when Tarini tried to convince her parents to agree to the union. Tarini's family were Brahmins, traditionally preachers and priests. They were, by profession, the most knowledgeable about the scriptures and religious practices of the Hindus and were revered by other castes. Socially, they considered themselves superior and hence unions with lower castes were never accepted. So when Tarini wrote to them, the family was upset and said that they would never accept a non-Brahmin, that too, a man from a scheduled tribe into the family. No amount of reasoning, persuasion or threat worked.

She rebelled. The couple got married without Tarini's parents' consent. Her in-laws, though, cooperated fully. A month later, she took her husband home after an overnight journey. His amiable and clean nature, depth of knowledge, gentle and suave manners attracted them to him. They gave him all the honour and love due to a son-in-law. A small reception was also organised and some of her relatives too came to bless the couple. A few guests, however, refused the invitation. When they returned, one of her uncles and a brother accompanied them, met Devendra's widowed mother and returned satisfied and happy.

As was the norm, she shifted to his house, and became a pivotal part of the family. His mother treated her as her own daughter, and a lasting relationship of love and trust grew between the two women. For seven long years, not a day passed when the mother would not stand at the gate, with a glass of cold water, to welcome her when she returned from office. When at home, she ensured her mother-in-law's comfort and did all the household chores. She washed her mother-in-law's clothes, combed her hair and gossiped about the happenings in office and in their neighbourhood.

'Those seven years were the best I experienced in my life. We had everything, materially and psychologically. It was love, joy and laughter, all in a simple thatched hut with huge courtyards in the front and rear,' recollected Tarini.

But tragedy stuck. Her mother-in-law's health deteriorated and she began to lose weight. She started spending most of her time in bed. If both Devendra and Tarini went to office, there was no one in the house to look after the bedridden woman. So when all her leave was exhausted, Tarini gave up her job. It was a difficult decision, but she considered it a small sacrifice to make for her wonderful mother-in-law who all along looked after her as if she was her own daughter.

One evening, she heard her mother-in-law lamenting, in whispers, to her son: 'You have given me everything. A very loving daughter-in-law, who is more than a daughter to me. But I will probably die without seeing the face of my grandchild.'

They had no progeny. They consulted a number of doctors at Guwahati and Calcutta. The final word from the doctors was a big blow to Tarini. She will not be able to bear a child because something was wrong with her ovaries. Tarini was shattered but put up a brave face in front of her husband. She was certain that the doctor's words must have had a devastating effect on her husband, but he never betrayed his feelings to her.

The mother-in-law's whispers made Tarini sit back and ponder. She spent sleepless nights thinking, with her husband mildly snoring by her side. Then she arrived at a solution.

The following day, she cycled a few miles to reach a village that came under her jurisdiction, when she was working. She knew a family there who had three marriageable daughters, the eldest eight years her junior. The family lived hand-to-mouth with the father always drunk. The mother and daughters did household jobs in the neighbourhood to earn a living. She had a long and persuasive chat with the mother. She came back with a straight yet triumphant face. Later that night, she hugged her husband and requested him for a favour. He unhesitatingly agreed.

Next, she asked him to promise not to say 'no'. Then she coyly whispered that she had found a girl who could beget a child. 'I want you to marry her,' she whispered. He looked into her eyes disbelievingly. Then he started crying like a child. Both cried together like babies.

Once they were sober, Devendra tried to argue, but she cut him short, reminding him of his promise. He kept trying to reason with her, but she was adamant. Devendra knew very well that if she had made up her mind, it was almost impossible to change it. So ultimately, he gave in after she argued that the arrangement would satisfy all, including his mother, him and specially her, because she was longing to cuddle his child.

Convincing the mother was a simple task. She reasoned with her that to nourish the family tree, her lone son must have a child. The only way forward for them was to have another woman in the family to carry Devendra's child. She argued that society will always accept such an arrangement for preserving the lineage.

In the entire plan, there was only one hitch: Hindu marriage law. The law stipulates that a Hindu man cannot have a second wife unless he divorces his first wife legally.

Devendra and his mother vehemently opposed a divorce. It was decided that the planned marriage would not be recorded in the official registry and in the documents at Devendra's office.

The marriage was solemnised in a simple ceremony and was attended by a few relatives and the couple's close friends. The bride was welcomed in the traditional manner by Tarini as the matriarch's health did not allow her to come out of her bed. Then something inauspicious happened. A gust of wind blew out the flickering flame of the earthen lamp that is customarily used for welcoming a new bride. Was this an ill omen?

At night when for the first time Tarini had to give away her bed to the newly-wed couple and sleep in a cot by the side of her mother-in-law, her heart ached. Two silent tears rolled down her cheeks.

Days and months went by. The new bride wasn't friendly. On the slightest pretext, she found fault with Tarini and picked up a fight. Tarini never retaliated or complained. The mother-in-law noticed it. She was upset, but refrained from interfering unless extreme provocation forced her to do so. When she did, the new daughter-in-law curtly told her not to meddle in her affairs. She was arrogant and positively rude.

Life carried on, but bad news brought gloom to the family. The mother-in-law was diagnosed with stomach cancer. An operation was immediately needed.

Simultaneously, another news cheered them up. The new bride was four months pregnant. This added a new responsibility on Tarini to look after her pre-natal care, with special focus on her food.

The operation was performed within a month at the Guwahati Cancer Hospital. It was followed by chemotherapy. The burden on Tarini and her husband was immense. The hospital was 100-odd km away. For a good fifteen days, Tarini attended to the patient in the hospital twenty-four hours a day, without rest.

To make matters worse, a few complications in the new bride's pregnancy required frequent consultations with the gynaecologist at Guwahati. Her husband's official commitments did not allow long absences. The only workable solution was to shift to Guwahati. They first hired accommodation at Guwahati and started living there. Subsequently, Tarini put all the money she had saved in eighteen years of her service life and bought a small piece of land there. They constructed a temporary shed and started living there. Later, they sold the ancestral farmland the family owned in the village and constructed a permanent house.

Her mother-in-law required hospitalisation every month for three days, post-surgery, for chemotherapy. Tarini and her husband shared the responsibilities of attending to the sick mother and to the pregnant woman at home, by turn. The pregnant woman was advised bed rest by the doctors for some complications. In addition, looking after the household jobs alone sapped Tarini's energy. However, she did not complain.

The family's joys knew no bounds when a male child was born. For the first time after a year, charged up by the happy news, the mother-in-law was able to walk unaided. She also tended to the newborn. Devendra bought plenty of fish and distributed it in the neighbourhood, as was the custom when a boy is born. For a baby girl, sweets are distributed. But alas! The merry-making was marred by a bizarre incident. The new mother would not allow Tarini to lift the child to take him in her lap. She believed that if a barren woman held a newborn in her lap, it would bring bad luck to the child.

Sadly enough, even the mother-in-law subscribed to this view. Tarini bore this ignominy silently, although her heart bled.

When the child was about a year old, the mother-in-law passed away. Both Tarini and Devendra wept like children, and for the first time in two years, clung to each other. About eight months later, Devendra sired another son. Tarini once again looked after the mother during the pregnancy. But her desire to cuddle the newborn was once again stonewalled by the mother.

Consequently, the two stepsons grew up trained to consider Tarini as an alien. When Devendra was around, the younger woman behaved as if she loved and respected

Tarini. But in his absence, she provoked and humiliated Tarini on the slightest pretext and squabbled over petty issues. Tarini endured the hostility and hatred silently. She did not want to trouble her husband. Their love and respect for each other was still so intense and the trust so complete that Tarini knew if she complained, he would not spare the second wife. So she never did. Sometimes, there were arguments on petty matters in front of him, but he regarded them as usual squabbles between two sisters. He was such a simpleton that he could not imagine that his young wife would ever be so ungrateful. But gradually, he realised what Tarini was going through silently and saw how the younger wife was always taking full advantage of his mild loving manner. He was especially agitated when the two young boys misbehaved with Tarini. He never spared them, then. That created a lot of commotion in the family, which he abhorred. However, when he found things were beyond repair, he toyed with the idea of separating from his younger wife. But before he could, something more challenging happened.

First, a painful eruption on Devendra's forehead lingered on long. It happened when the eldest son was ten. Tarini, who believed in black magic, was certain it was the result of a neighbour's ill will towards her family. Her suspicions were confirmed when the swelling did not subside even after a doctor's medication. A few months later, a similar eruption appeared on his chin.

An occult practitioner from a nearby village was summoned who prescribed herbal potions for application on his entire body. After three months, many more eruptions that were even more painful appeared on the lower limbs.

Tarini took him to a leading dermatologist, but nothing worked. Then she took him to a Kolkata hospital. The prolonged treatment and medication cost them his life's savings. For three years, he had been unable to attend office.

With five mouths to feed, expenses on medicines and doctor's fees and the education of the two boys, life became an uphill journey. Tarini worked in her spare time, and even sold his ancestral home. The family hit rock bottom.

Meanwhile, Devendra was in pain and agony. He had become a living skeleton. According to Tarini, the doctors could not diagnose what was wrong. She ran from pillar to post looking for a solution, but nothing worked. Then, as a last resort, someone suggested that she take him to the Christian Medical College, Vellore, a three-day train journey away.

She estimated she would need at least Rs 150,000. In addition, she would have to cater for the other members of the family left behind. She had no money.

She made several trips to his office as well as to the

office of the state's Director of Health Services. There was no provision in the government's rulebook to sanction expenditure for treatment of staff in a private hospital.

The last option was to sell half of the plot they had purchased earlier at Guwahati, on which they built their house in one corner. The younger wife protested but the land was in Tarini's name. Tarini sold half of the plot for Rs 2 lakh.

In a fortnight, she set off for Vellore in a first class coupe. He required support at every step. 'Taking him to the toilet in a moving train was most challenging as people were hesitant to touch him because of the eruptions all over his body,' said Tarini.

At Vellore, he was hospitalised for three months. His condition deteriorated and nothing seemed to help. 'Was it cancer?' I asked her, directly. She replied with a curt, 'Maybe'.

In three months, alone in an alien city, she tended to him, night and day. 'I was completely sleep-deprived,' she said to me. 'I must have lost half my weight with no proper food or rest'.

But her love and respect for the man who had been her companion, her soulmate and guide, the man who had gone out of his way to keep her happy, and given her all the respect and love, egged her on. She never complained and instead devoted herself to the thought that one day, he will be cured and be able to walk again with her, hand-in-hand, reminiscing about their joyful past.

Her hopes were shattered when the doctors gave up and advised her to take him back. By that time, he was absolutely emaciated, almost like a skeleton and was unable to breathe properly. She knew his days were numbered. She decided that he must see his children before he died. So she hired a cab and with help from the hospital staff, put him in and started for Chennai, from where she planned to take the train to Guwahati.

At Chennai railway station, she made him comfortable on a bench, then left to reserve the berth for Guwahati. After the bookings, she returned to find him struggling for breath. Then he suddenly gasped and within seconds, he was no more. A policeman found her sobbing uncontrollably clinging to his body. When he discovered what had happened, the police organised the funeral and she consigned his mortal remains to flames according to the Hindu tradition. Except for two policemen and the priest, no one else attended the funeral. The good policeman offered her a place to stay for the night, but she preferred to be dropped off at the station.

Next evening, she took the train to Guwahati.

'I had never felt so lonely in my life. The world crumbled around me. I even thought of jumping out of the train to commit suicide. Perhaps, that would have been the best decision of my life. However, I refrained because I thought I had other responsibilities. I decided

I would work to realise his dream of making the two boys into good human beings. I would make the mother realise that it would be our combined effort to bring up the children.'

Reaching home, there were surprises galore. There was a stranger at home, the local goon. There was no sign of gloom in the house. The father's death had not affected the children. The eldest was out of the house. The younger, now in his teens, was playing merrily with other children. The wife was dressing up to go somewhere with the stranger. All of them ignored her.

She expected the elder son to be at home in a white dress eating only fruits and soaked gram the whole day and an evening meal of rice and lentils without oil till the eleventh-day ritual was over. It was the custom. But he was nowhere to be seen. After a while, he came home dressed in jeans, and showed no signs of grief or respect to the departed. Tarini could not stand this complete disrespect and disregard for her beloved departed husband who was their father. She erupted like a volcano, admonishing him and commanded him to dress up in whites as a mark of respect to his father.

This infuriated the boy and his mother. She was tersely told to mind her own business and to refrain from meddling in the affairs of the house. The mother went to the extent of alleging that Tarini had slow-poisoned her husband, and then taken him to Vellore to kill him. That was the last nail in the coffin. A tumultuous, no holds barred, nasty and acrimonious battle followed thereafter for more than two years, culminating in physical assaults by the mother and children on Tarini. Worse was to follow. The mother and sons threw her out of her own house built on her own land.

The goon, in fact, was the person who instigated the three to evict her forcefully. There was yet another twist in the story. According to Tarini's own account, an FIR was lodged in the local police station alleging Tarini was running a flesh trade business from the house because of which they evicted her. I have intentionally not verified any of the happenings narrated above, but I am nevertheless penning them down because as the reader will discover subsequently, this has a lot to do with Tarini's psychological problems, which we tried to cure.

A retired engineer brought Tarini to Seneh in June 2013. He told us that she had no shelter or means of livelihood and was found begging in the area where he lived. He also told us that she actually had a house not very far from his house but some local goons evicted her forcefully from it. He and some of his neighbours had tried to intervene, but the police was against her and hence they gave up. He also told us that she was fighting a legal battle to receive the family pension of her deceased husband. Later, we contacted her lawyer who said he was trying for an out-of-court settlement, as the judgement was getting inordinately delayed. He said the case was very much in Tarini's favour, since she was the legal wife according to the records produced.

We did not have the resources to help Tarini in her legal battle, except for deputing one of our nurses to accompany her to meet her lawyer. Later, we were told that the case had been settled and she had finally earned some compensation. Since we provide absolutely free shelter, food, clothing, and medical facilities to our residents, we wilfully avoid any account of their personal finances, if any. To the best of our knowledge, none of the residents have any money or assets whatsoever.

Tarini was a multifaceted personality. She was a staunch believer in black magic and it was a challenge to us to convince her to go to the doctor, since she thought all ailments can be cured better by the sorcerers.

Thus, when she had arthritis, she insisted on visiting a quack whom she believed could simply cure her by chanting some mantras and sprinkling water with some fern leaves placed on her joints. Again, when the doctor found her to be diabetic, she first refused allopathic medication. It was only with lots of persuasion that our nurses were able to make her swallow the pills prescribed for her diabetes.

She was an expert cook and a wizard in chanting religious hymns. She led the morning and afternoon prayers with her archive of devotional songs that were stored in her brain. The way she blessed the gathering in a religious congregation was a treat to watch and hear.

Long after her story was penned, Tarini breathed her last due to renal failure. All efforts made to save her life with regular daily dialysis and medication went in vain. She was cremated in the presence of a large gathering with the last rites performed by one of our nurses. Her memory still haunts me, for I had failed to take her to her ancestral home she wanted to visit. She requested me for it a number of times.

Just before she died, two of her relatives came to visit her in the hospital. They also attended her funeral but did not perform the last rites. She had a good sum in her bank account. We handed over the bank papers retrieved from her belongings to them. We do not know whether they claimed the money. It positively was none of our concern.

Shefali

A Tale Of Displacement

If true, Shefali's story, as narrated by her is bound to raise your hackles because of the sheer cruelty of fate. I must confess, despite my best efforts, I could not ascertain its truthfulness. She could not offer me any lead to anyone who knew her to throw some light about her past.

She is all alone in this world. From whatever I have seen during our association of several years, she is a very pious, soft-spoken lady with a heart of gold, non-interfering and non complaining by nature, one who always praises others. This itself gives me ample justification to believe that the story of her life, as told by her, is true. In fact, whenever I confronted her with some contradictions in her narrations that took place over the course of a few months, she would hit her head with her withered palm and mutter, 'Oh Ma! What has happened to my memory? How can I forget my past?'

Let me start with her childhood. Shefali's father worked as an assistant to a zamindar, an affluent landlord, in the days of undivided Bengal, long before the bifurcation of the country on religious lines. Life was honky dory with her parents and there was always plenty to eat and enough to live on, thanks to the largesse of their kind and considerate landlord. They even had enough for some small luxuries. Apart from her father, her two maternal uncles also worked in the same estate. Shefali was the second of three siblings.

Atrocities fanned by religious bigots who whipped up communal passions on the eve of Partition affected the simple peasants and the poor ruthlessly, from both sides of the religious divide. Family lives of many were completely devastated. Both communities spoke the same language and shared a rich culture, a similar way of living, literature, music, dance and food habits. But for a lone occasional skull cap and the flowing beard of the older members, there was no way to even differentiate who practised which religion.

The two communities had lived for centuries as one civilisation, in complete harmony, with only minor aberrations. In the countryside, the landlords were predominantly Hindu and their tillers mostly Muslims who formed the majority community in undivided Bengal. However, post-Partition, the fire of hatred had spread like wildfire, singeing every community and eclipsing all humane considerations and sanity.

One fateful day, a motley crowd of armed men from the majority community swooped down upon them, killing her two uncles who tried to save the zamindar and his family.

The frenzied crowd torched the landlord's house and looted all his belongings. The zamindar fled with his wife and children. In absolute panic, Shefali's family also fled with nothing but the clothes they wore and a few rupees that her father had saved. The journey was arduous and treacherous and they had to walk mostly at night to avoid the hostile crowds. The area was inhospitable because of the monsoons and the deep foliage.

To cross the rivers, they had to hire boats. The crafty boatmen charged up to eight annas each for a 10-minute ride to cross the rivers of the delta, eight times the amount they charged in normal times. It was a huge amount to dole out in those days, for one could buy a week's ration with that amount for a family of two. But they had no choice but to pay up. Exhausted, they camped on the shores of the rivers, hiding among the foliage. They had no protection against the torrential rains that lashed unannounced, every now and then. The thunder would shake their terrified spirits. They were scared of the lightning, for it might expose them to the angry crowds, who wandered around menacingly to spot and kill members of the opposite community.

After eight days of walking and crossing a number of rivers that flowed en route, the family finally reached safer areas inhabited mostly by Hindus in Assam's Karimganj district. They lived in a dingy relief camp in tattered tents in an unhygienic environment until they were driven out to accommodate new arrivals. The camp provided one meal a day. The rest, they had to manage themselves by purchasing grains from the local market at exorbitant prices and cook in a corner of the tent. Life was hard but they were safe.

From the camp at Karimganj, the family travelled by train to Guwahati where they lived in a shanty near the railway tracks with a few others. By that time, her parents had exhausted all the money they had. Her father tried to make a living by working as a daily labourer with a contractor. He had no experience of physical labour and was slow and lethargic, inviting ire and disdain from the contractor, who used to scold him every now and then. But the two-anna coin he earned every day was necessary for their survival, so he swallowed his ego and lumbered on.

Work was difficult to find. Begging was an option, but there were more beggars than donors. The three siblings scavenged used cans or whatever they could lay their hands on. They sold the fruits of their day's labour, and it would fetch them a few paise. Even here, there was stiff competition from others like themselves, who had lost everything they had to the religious frenzy.

The struggle for survival was an ordeal in itself. Their makeshift tarpaulin-roofed hut would leak profusely when rains lashed them. On such days, work was almost impossible to get and food was scarce. The twigs Shefali collected from the nearby shrubs for lighting the hearth were wet and refused to burn. Her dark skin would get auburn with the rush of blood to her tender face as she tried to blow air through the bamboo pipe that her father had made for the purpose. If the rains did not stop for a few days, the only food they had was a handful of puffed rice with water. On such days, the family clung to each other like baby caterpillars. Except for the frequent sighs of anguish displayed by her mother and the occasional squabbles between the siblings, their lives had only one aim: to survive on whatever they could lay their hands on.

But, fate had more severe plans ahead for them. An epidemic of smallpox spread like wildfire in the cluster of shacks they lived in. She lost her eldest brother to it. Her younger brother survived with marks criss-crossing his tender face, almost disfiguring him. After a few months, he had an attack of pneumonia. There was no money for medicines, and one day, an unabated bout of coughing robbed him of his life.

They cried, the mother clutching her to her bosom, and the father howling like a wounded canine until hunger pangs and the realities of their need to survive made the father go searching for a job. Fate was indeed cruel. They were even denied time to grieve, leave alone find comfort on a compassionate shoulder of a friend or relative.

The life shattered like a piece of glass, the family decided to move away from Guwahati to a nearby town. There, they hired a one-room hut with a thatched roof and embarked on a new life. The father got a job as a salesman in a grocery shop and the mother found a job as a part-time help in an affluent household. Shefali became the apple of their eyes, the parents succumbing to all her demands as a teenager and spent sleepless nights, in sheer agony, if she was even slightly indisposed. A common cold triggered panic. The bond between the three became stronger.

Teen Shefali had no window available to go to school. As she grew up into a young woman, she started going with her mother to help her in her job as a domestic help. She also earned for her exclusive job of looking after the toddler of their employer, a good sumptuous lunch every day and a couple of rupees at the end of the month. With three of them earning, life became comfortable. Some earnings were kept aside, every month, for Shefali's eventual marriage.

At sixteen, Shefali fell in love with a small-time contractor who lived with his old parents in a nearby locality. With high cheekbones, a somewhat flat nose, a pair of bright brown eyes and a thin moustache, he was a handsome young man of twenty-five. When I try to visualise a sixteen-year-old Shefali in her prime, I imagine a tall, slim, dark-skinned girl with a pair of intense eyes. Her prominent forehead culminated in a long nose that ended abruptly to accommodate two comparatively large nostrils and a mouth with heavy lips, the bottom one thicker than the other, with two rows of finely crafted teeth, white and shining, the top incisors a little protruding.

I am sure, she must have had a luxurious tuft of long hair falling down to her waist, black and wavy, like the tail of a black race horse, because even today it looks lustrous.

With the tacit permission of the elders of both the families, the courtship lasted for six months until they were married on a rainy day in August. 'The umbrella held on top of the groom to ward off the rains could not stop the damage to his headgear which was made of compressed paper fibre. It got completely wet and crumpled when the bridegroom was received by my mother, forcing his best man to remove it from his head,' recalled Shefali. Eyewitnesses narrated his plight to her since she was not allowed to come out to receive him.

Shefali's mother-in-law was very kind and comforting and immediately took her under her wings like a bird gathering her chicks, and took it upon herself to teach her all the nuances of married life, trying her best to fill the void created by the absence of Shefali's parents. 'She was so considerate and loving! I tried my best not to betray my tender feelings towards my own parents, lest she feel my love for her was comparatively less,' Shefali said.

Life was tough for the family. Her in-laws were old without any independent means of livelihood. The only income was what Shefali's husband earned from his business as a sub-contractor and the occasional small remittances from their married older son who lived in a town on the hills. He worked as a peon in a government office in Shillong. Her husband spent all day supervising the small part of a job that the main contractor passed on to him at a rate much lower than sanctioned by the government. The little money he earned was hardly sufficient to meet the family's expenses. The earnings were not steady and sometimes, there was no work for months.

The soft-spoken, non-complaining Shefali, who had seen much hardship in life, was happy that she had a loving husband and wonderful in-laws. They never went without food, like in her teenage years. When the women of the neighbourhood visited her in-laws, they were eloquent about her looks and amiable nature. Shefali's heart would jump in happiness and she would run to her room at the earliest opportunity and swirl like a Turkish Huron dancer in front of the mirror to express her joy.

Young Shefali's only obsession in those days was to sit in front of the mirror and admire her own smile. Even today, her smile is captivating. Her broad heavy lips arch upwards and the muscles around her mouth contract, creating two distinct arcs on both sides of the mouth. Now at around seventy-five, although sickness and lack of sleep sap her and the pain on her ankles and knees torment her, making movement painful, her lips get dry and her eyes further recede into their furrows, the broad grin does not ever leave her face.

She always presents herself dressed well. Visitors to Seneh will invariably find Shefali in a neat cotton sari, immaculately worn, one end of it covering her head, like any other traditional Bengali housewife, her signature smile hanging at all times on her lips.

After 18 months of marriage, Shefali delivered a baby boy. The healthy boy became the focus of prime attention from everyone in the family. With his coming, whatever void they had felt in life, so far, vanished. It was joy, joy and joy, all the way, and time for celebrations. His birth was celebrated with much fanfare. The family threw a lavish party and the guest list included friends of her husband and in-laws, and her own parents. Holding the baby to her bosom, her mother cried in happiness. Her normally withdrawn and reserved father betrayed his feelings with a bear hug to Shefali. He then lifted the baby carefully as if it was an object of fragile glass, all the while a broad grin lighting up his wrinkled face.

Two weeks on, her father died of a heart attack, before any medical intervention could be arranged.

The baby grew up to be a toddler and then a mischievous four-year-old. Shefali's mother-in-law suffered from arthritis and was confined to her bed, so the responsibility of running the entire household fell on her shoulders. There was no time for rest throughout the day. Luckily, she enjoyed a robust health.

But her husband's fortunes weren't robust at all. With stiff competition from others who had joined his profession lately, he barely got work. Even if he did, returns were low. He decided to try his luck at Shillong on his brother's advice. Shefali stayed back to take care of her in-laws.

In about a year, her mother-in-law expired. Shefali's husband picked up a job as an accountant in a small plywood factory at Shillong. He decided to shift the family to Shillong.

The two brothers hired two small neighbouring units in a Bengali-dominated locality. They had a common kitchen. Life was smooth initially. Her elder sister-in-law took a liking to Shefali and they all lived together as one happy family. The young boy was growing well in the loving care of the family, together with his two young cousins. However, Shillong's cold and wet climate never suited her father-in-law. Severe respiratory problems robbed him of his life within one year.

To add to her problems, her brother-in-law shifted to a free government accommodation located far away, two months after the demise of the old man.

Thus Shefali, for the first time, started living alone with her nuclear family. The initial days were smooth with a caring husband, a young son who demanded her full attention at all times, and a comfortable income.

When it is not raining, Shillong has a wonderful salubrious climate. At times, she would sing loudly all alone and try to mimic the sounds of the birds in the trees. Occasionally, she would lower her *pallu* and feel the breeze caress her bare skin. Life had never been so good for the thirty-five-year-old Shefali. 'I thought God had ultimately opened His loving eyes on me,' she told me.

But alas, the old adage, 'Man proposes, God disposes,' came true for her. Initially she had suspected nothing when her husband came home, an hour or more later than normal. She would wait eagerly for him to return, to serve him a cup of hot tea that he was so fond of. Gradually, the delays became longer. When asked for the reason for the delay, he evaded a direct answer.

Occasionally, her husband was in the habit of having a drink or two with his friends. She had never protested. It was his way of enjoyment, she reasoned. But lately, his drinking bouts increased. Often, he came home tipsy. If she protested, he would become abusive. Later some shoving and a slap or two became the order of the day. Shefali's instinct told her that something else would be the reason. She begged a neighbour to spy on him.

He did. What he found was devastating. Her entire body shook like a jungle deer, caught live. She cried uncontrollably, clasping her ten-year-old son to her bosom, sobbing and kissing him hard. Sensing something was amiss, the poor boy started crying too.

The neighbour had brought the information that her husband was seeing a woman who lived in a suburb on the way to his office. The lady was a local tribal widow, around thirty-five years of age. She was an attractive, fair woman. Shefali, on the other hand, was copper-coloured. It is no secret that most Indian males, even today, have a weakness for fair-skinned women.

The local tribal populace despised outsiders and seldom mingled with them. There was a divide in religion also. A majority of the Khasis and Jayantias as they are known, were Christians. Unlike the outsiders who had migrated to the hills, their ancestors had lived there for centuries with their distinct and exclusive cultures and dialects. They were very possessive about them.

The people from the plains had come in large numbers, after the British came to India, and made Shillong the capital of undivided Assam. They allowed settlements of

East Bengalis and others in large numbers in Shillong to help them administer the state as clerks and petty officials. The tribal inhabitants resented this silent invasion. The sparingly populated original inhabitants of the entire hilly terrain that constituted the Khasi and Jayantia district, had their distinct culture and social order. The only contact they had with outsiders was with the neighbouring Assamese ethnic groups, who never attempted to occupy their land until the British intervened.

The locals resented Shefali's husband hobnobbing with one of their women. They threatened him a number of times and twice waylaid him. But wine and women had become his weakness. The lady, too, encouraged him to visit her. He was caught between the devil and the deep sea. On the one hand was his caring and loving wife, for whom he and the son were her world. She loved him whole-heartedly, met all his needs, and cared for him as only a simple-natured, submissive wife can do. She never displayed her frustration or anger. On top of it, their only son, a handsome, mischievous lean boy was the apple of their eyes. He wholeheartedly loved the kid.

Matters came to a boil when local goons attacked and beat him up. They gave him only one choice: to desert his wife for good and shift to his paramour's house with his son and marry her or face the consequences (the Khasis are a matriarchal society) and be prepared to die. His paramour had no children from her previous marriage. Till then, Shefali's husband was considering his relationship with the woman as a mere pastime.

Now he found himself in a quagmire. The only option was to flee.

It was a cold, foggy December morning. Strong winds made a dreary sound as they swept through the empty branches of the pine trees. They had taken only what they could carry with them. They boarded an early morning bus to the plains, the three of them huddled together. The bus rolled on and picked up speed. Around twenty-odd minutes later, as they began to relax, and Shefali was in the process of opening her bags to take out some food, the bus came to a shrieking halt. All of a sudden, a few drunken youths armed with deadly machetes and sticks barged in through the front door. They walked menacingly towards them. Sensing danger, Shefali's husband dashed towards the rear door. But he was caught.

While narrating the story to me, Shefali suddenly started sobbing aloud. Her hands trembled, and her head shook. In a broken voice she said, 'Sir, the ghastly murder of my husband in front my own eyes gives me nightmares even today. Quite often I wake up at night, sobbing, with my heart pounding wildly.' The occupant of the bed next to her has been complaining about Shefali's loud nightmares that disturb her frequently.

Her husband was chopped into pieces in front of

her with all the other passengers watching mutely in horror. He was wriggling like a fish out of water while there was still life in his body. Blood spewed out from everywhere. His shrieks were heart shattering, but within a few minutes, his mangled torso lay still. The last word he uttered was 'Mago', a Bengali word when a distressed child calls out to his mother. The women and the children in the bus shrieked in terror.

Shefali did not know what happened thereafter. She had fainted. The co-passengers on the bus attended on her. When she regained consciousness and came out of her stupor, the bus had halted at a crowded place. She tried to look for her son. He was not there. The others told her that the murderers had forcibly taken him away with them. The boy had cried aloud trying to hang onto the unconscious body of his mother, but his feeble resistance was silenced easily with a hard slap.

Later, the police came. The local police had no jurisdiction over the area where the murder had been committed. So, they informed the concerned police station about the crime. They also recorded the statements of a few reluctant eyewitnesses. Shefali never heard anything about what happened to either the case or the boy.

Some ten years thence, someone told her that the boy had grown up and was staying with his foster mother, the woman her husband had courted.

Apparently, he had adapted to his new environment, and even spoke the dialect of his foster mother and attended church regularly. He appeared happy. It did not look like he missed his real mother.

This was the sad and grotesque saga of Shefali's past. But her ordeal did not end there. Her struggle to survive actually started thereafter. After the ghastly murder, she landed up with her mother who had shifted to Guwahati and started life anew after the demise of her father. The mother had a small shack constructed on a small piece of government land atop a hillock. The one-room accommodation had barely enough space for a single bed and a small fireplace in the corner with three bricks to hold a saucepan over the flame where she cooked her meals with firewood. The utensils were stacked on a wooden rack not very far from the fireplace. Her clothes hung on a rope tied across the width of the shack. She worked as a part-time maid in two houses on the foot hills, earning just enough to make both ends meet.

Shefali was devastated and a mental wreck because of the trauma she had gone through. The shack had no space for two beds, so the mother-daughter duo decided to move the bed out and sleep on the floor. The moment Shefali would close her eyes, the horrible scene would haunt her and she would start weeping uncontrollably. All through the day, she would gaze vacantly, murmuring incoherently.

Her mother was at her wit's end. It was dangerous for her to leave Shefali alone at home and go for work. So after a week, she started taking Shefali along to share her workload. As her expenses had gone up, she took up work in other households as well. It required quite an effort for her mother to make Shefali work since she was habitually lazy and lethargic. She abhorred swabbing the floors since it required bending on all fours. With time, she got used to it and stopped whining. Exhausted by the day's labour, she started sleeping better, too. Only occasionally would nightmares disturb her.

Thus Shefali started a new life. Every morning, both mother and daughter left together, to work in different houses. Shefali's limbs finally got accustomed to the rigour. With both of them earning, sustenance became easy. They even managed to replace their tarpaulin roof with a cast iron corrugated sheet. A small kitchen was added to the main structure. They also replaced their makeshift, jute cloth-enclosed, open-to-the-sky, toilet with a tin roof and bamboo walls.

Life went by smoothly until Shefali's ageing mother got sick frequently. She became incapable of going out to work. To ensure their income remained steady, Shefali started working additionally in the households hitherto served by her mother. It meant working from dawn to sunset; she went out early morning for work, trekked back uphill at lunch time to eat her food, then went back to work after a brief rest. In the fifth year of such an existence, Shefali's mother, who was by then completely bedridden, died.

Shefali was forty-eight and had already lost some of her jobs as she had to tend to her mother in her final days. Most of her old employers had already employed new helps. Shefali had to find new jobs. But the area where she picked her jobs was far away. Returning home for lunch became untenable, so she went out in the mornings and returned home exhausted in the evening.

A kind employer gave her lunch regularly. At her house, she met a police officer who suggested that she move into his house as a full-time maid. Her jobs would include housekeeping and helping his wife in the cooking. In return, she was promised comfortable accommodation with a fan, food, clothing, medical care if needed, and an attractive pay.

So, at the age of fifty-two, she shifted to his home. The officer kept his promise, his wife was considerate, and their children accepted her as a part of their family. Ultimately, Shefali got a home and some nice people to live with. Her mild manners, her patience, willingness to accept faults immediately when pointed out, and her humility endeared her to all. Shefali stayed there until she turned sixty-two when once again, fate played truant. She developed arthritis. The household chores became a challenge. From being an asset, she became a liability to the family.

Sometime in June 2014, we received a call from a retired police officer informing us that he wanted to meet us to get help for an old, sick woman. The next day, he came, a portly man around sixty plus with a bulging belly. He made up a nice story of finding Shefali in his neighbourhood and offering her a home out of compassion. However, it was not possible for him to look after her indefinitely. He requested us to accommodate her in our home for destitute old women. We were moved by his humanitarian act, appreciated his efforts and despatched a nurse and a help to go find out if what he had told us was true.

They went to his house and the lady of the house ushered them into a small room where a woman was sleeping on a bed. She appeared sick. Our team came back satisfied. We requested the gentleman to bring her over to Seneh.

He came the next day with Shefali. My first impression was that Shefali did not look very sick and positively did not look starved. She was fat, very slow in her movements and was quite affable. After the mandatory paperwork, the gentleman left, leaving Shefali behind. Later when she was confident that fate had brought her to the right place, she told us the actual story. Shefali had worked in their house for a little over eleven years, but for the last six months, because of her arthritis and physical debility, she was unable to perform her duties regularly. In fact, she admitted, she had become a liability to the family. Hence, they had decided to abandon her.

We sent her to a local hospital for examination and evaluation of her problems. After a series of tests including a bone density test, the doctors opined that she had multiple physical conditions. She had arthritis, was diabetic, anaemic as well as hypertensive.

She was put on medication straightway. Now the blood pressure and the diabetes are under control. Her arthritis and anaemia remain a cause of worry. Initially, both improved and she started helping others in odd jobs. But with advancing age, she has become dependent on others and sometimes, she requires support when she walks.

Shefali remains an enigma to us. She went through insurmountable turmoil, horror and suffering. But she is able to bury her past. She displays a remarkable forbearance. Nothing seems to ruffle her. She has learnt to live for today, in perfect mental peace, leaving behind the past as a series of bad dreams. Her inspiring broad smile that never leaves her lips tells it all.

Roma

A Victim Of Her Own Silent World

Tall and elegant, dark-complexioned, with flowing eyebrows, hollowed bright-grey eyes, high cheekbones, a prominent nose and an elongated mouth when closed giving the impression of the arc of a bow, the upper lip parted in the middle with a comparatively deep gorge, Roma was brought to us by a smartly dressed, seemingly well-bred middle-aged lady. The lady said she found Roma near her house, squatting on the pavement, lost and bewildered, weak and hungry, unable even to remember where she was from, or even who she was.

The lady took her home, gave her shelter and looked after her. She was in their house for a few months. Her husband, however, did not approve of her compassion and insisted she must turn her out of the house. She tried hard to find a suitable place to accommodate her, and even asked for help from the police, who sent her to a shelter home run by the government. The place was dingy and dirty, with hardly any supervision. She decided against abandoning her there. So, she asked help from a high-profile woman politician known to her, who referred her to one of our lady trustees.

The trustee believed her story and commended her for her show of compassion; she organised her stay in Seneh.

Roma who looked around seventy-plus, thus, became a resident. We discovered she was stone deaf and could hardly see. She was so weak that she could not walk without support. There was no way to communicate with her other than by sign language. Her replies were feeble and scanty. After a few days' stay, while trying to give her a bath, our support staff noticed tell-tale marks of recent torture on her body.

The doctors certified that the marks were caused by beating. We tried to contact the lady on the mobile number she gave us, but repeated calls remained unanswered. We informed the police in writing about this and also wrote a letter to the address of the lady who had brought her to us. We did not hear of any action by the police nor from her.

We decided to give up on both and instead

concentrated on nursing Roma back to health. With about two weeks of nursing and regular food, Roma could walk unsupported. She also started talking. Her voice was neither strong nor weak or soft, but a little husky and easily audible, giving the impression of a coherent speaker. Later, we got both her eyes operated, giving a gap of a month between the two surgeries. Then she could see and read with the spectacles we provided.

One day, unexpectedly, she started speaking to the nurse attending on her about the history of the Mughals. The nurse had no knowledge about history, leave alone the Mughal empire. We were astounded. Because of her hearing impairment, we could not communicate with her, so I wrote down in English if she knew the language. She astounded us all by replying in English, 'Of course. Why not? I used to teach in English and in Assamese, both.'

That is how we gradually came to know her version of the sad saga of her life. What she narrated sometimes vocally, and sometimes in writing, sent shivers down our spines. Can men be so cruel? Can our society be so apathetic and devoid of humane feelings? Can greed make men stoop so low? Are we a civilised society? Can God be so partisan? Can fate be so ruthless? These questions remain unanswered in my mind.

I have seen both facets of human behaviour—the kind and the just, and the cruel and the ruthless. Unfortunately, even in how God decides the fate or destiny of a person, there is always a dichotomy. The more we rummage into a person's sufferings, the more confused we get about the uncertainties of life and about how the Almighty dispenses justice.

Coming back to Roma, I must apprise the readers in the first instance, that Roma's thought process was a bit jumbled. She was extremely moody. At times, she was eloquent and clear. On other occasions, depending on her mood, her answers were monosyllabic, leaving enough room for alternative interpretations.

I intentionally did not research much to verify her story at length, except finding out the route she treaded in her life. This is what I discovered. I am not vouching for the authenticity of every statement that I am making. I have tried to fill in the gaps with some of the unverified information she supplied to us and, at times, with my own imagination.

Born to a middle-class Bengali family, Roma was a very hard-working and diligent student. She did her BA with history as her major, passing with distinction and then joined the University of Guwahati to do her MA in history. She completed it with a first class. 'I was the tallest girl in my class,' she once told me in reply to my query about her University days. 'When I decided to close-crop my hair short, everyone complimented me as the most attractive girl in my class,' she said.

When I imagine a twenty-something Roma, I see

a tall, slim, shapely woman with sharp features, with taut, ebony-coloured unblemished skin, her hair neatly cropped, covering her ears, draped elegantly in a simple sari, staring at me intently with a pair of very bright eyes. She must have been a very attractive young woman! To top it all, if her academic record as claimed by her is taken into account, she, indeed, was very intelligent. A beauty with brains.

Before her MA final results were declared, Roma got an offer for a lecturership in Biswanath Charali College, a reputed college of yesteryears that produced quite a few famous alumni. She taught history with gusto and confidence. She was a teacher with a no-nonsense attitude. From what I gathered from talking to one of her students, now a senior state government employee who lives in Guwahati, Roma was a strict but genial teacher.

She was a popular professor, her students idolised her, peers were very fond of her geniality and admired her intellect. She had a special relationship with Prof Goswami, probably a peer, who was more than a friend to her he was her mentor, guide, ideal and probably much more. Here I am hazarding a guess, since on her last days, in delirium, she quite often would announce, 'Oh dear. At last, Professor Goswami has come to take me.'

However, her parents got her married to a young executive who was the area manager of Usha Industries. He was a bright, smart, suave man. H was very fond of her. She did not give up her teaching job after marriage. Since he was posted in Guwahati, they would visit each other every weekend by turn to spend time together. She looked forward to the long holidays when she would travel to Guwahati where he had rented a small accommodation.

At the slightest opportunity, they would travel together to Shillong, a few hours' bus journey from Guwahati, and enjoy the togetherness, the weather, the beauty of the evergreen hills and the song of the pines when its leaves dance in the ever-present breeze. It was a life of love and bliss, of bondage and togetherness, of understanding and mutual dependence.

However, fate had other plans for Roma. One day, she woke up with a terrible pain in both her ears. The local doctor gave her some drops, but these did not help. Within days, she discovered a sharp decline in her hearing capabilities. Accompanied by her husband, she went from one specialist to another in Guwahati and Kolkata but the condition only deteriorated, till she couldn't hear at all. Her husband took her to CMC Vellore, the premiere medical college and hospital of India those days, where the doctors declared that she would never be able to hear again. She came back to the college, but found that she was unable to communicate with her students. She was forced to leave her job.

Back in Guwahati, her husband gave her strength to

cope with this sad turn of events. But, once again, fate played truant. One fine morning, her husband woke up with a terrible headache and blurred vision, followed by high temperature. He was rushed to the hospital, but within days, he breathed his last, dying of the deadly cerebral malaria.

The world crumbled around her like an inadequately cemented brick wall. Earlier, she had lost both her parents. She had no siblings. She had no offspring. She had no money and no roof over her head. To top it all, she was stone deaf. After the mourning period, she started looking for a job. No one was interested in hiring her. Ultimately, her brother-in-law took her along to Burdhwan, a small town near Kolkata, to live with him. He was a kind and considerate man who tried to give her comfort and a family life. The trouble was his wife, who resented her presence and would hurt her constantly with her deeds and attitude. To add fuel to the fire, Roma was habitually lazy and abhorred physical work. She certainly was a burden to her sister-in-law. With passing days, her life became unbearable. Gradually, she started losing her strength of mind and spirit. There was a discernible change in her behaviour as she became withdrawn and melancholic.

Her brother-in-law decided, for the sake of his family's peace, he will have to get Roma out of the house. He left her in a home for destitute women. According to Roma, her sister-in-law usurped all her belongings, including her ornaments.

Roma had a comparatively good life in the home. She jelled well with the other residents. The home was run by an elderly gentleman who was kind, chivalrous and understanding. She lived there for ten long years, but once again, fate took a cruel turn.

One day, the good Samaritan died after a brief ailment. His heirs closed the destitute home. She was thrown out on the streets. In the interim, her brother in-law also died. The sister-in-law would not entertain her. Roma had nowhere to go. Her niece took pity on her and brought Roma to Guwahati. The niece lived in a flat with her husband and daughter, but unfortunately, the niece had a strained relationship with her husband. Roma's presence in the house became yet another bone of contention. On the slightest pretext, he tortured Roma and tried to throw her out of the house. This further complicated the relationship between the husband and the wife. Finally, the lady decided to find an alternative.

To be fair, the lady was helpless. She had first gone to the police station for help. As an act of abundant precaution, she never told the police about Roma's real identity and had told them that she had picked up Roma from the streets. She did not like the place the police recommended. As a final resort, she brought Roma to Seneh. A cursory look at Roma was enough to convince us she needed help.

The niece did not tell us they were related. She actually cooked up the story about finding Roma on the road.

Later we came to know her intention was noble. She wanted to look after Roma but her husband never allowed it. He forced her to get rid of Roma. That explained why she took Roma first to the police station next to the government run Destitute Home and finally to Seneh. In all probability, the husband was in the habit of torturing Roma.

On arrival, Roma looked extremely pale and fragile. She kept quiet, not uttering a word. When we approached her, she gazed at our faces intently with suspicion and apprehension. Since she was totally hearing impaired, there was no way to communicate verbally with her. She looked so scared and timid we never imagined that she was a highly educated teacher. The lady had left in a hurry after signing the mandatory papers. Later, it turned out, the address she wrote on the papers was fake.

Weeks passed and Roma's health improved. She became cheerful and energetic. Her confidence in herself came back. She would advise others about good behaviour and the need to maintain decorum. She would quite often flaunt her intellectual superiority with monologues about discipline. Others, at times, did not take her words calmly. And because of her absolute hearing impairment, she was not aware of how others reacted. We tried hard to make her understand that she must behave as one among equals and participate in all activities as a team member.

As a rule, the residents of Seneh cook food for all, clean the utensils, sweep and swab the area, clean the toilets, maintain and nurse the flower beds according to a roster, by turn. Roma abhorred physical work and no amount of counselling, cajoling, or persuasion resulted in motivating her to do any work. She initially even refused to make her own bed, let alone undertake common jobs. This resulted in several protests from others. But Roma did not budge.

She became a challenge to the support staff. We counselled them to be patient and to handle Roma with kid gloves. It helped. Roma finally started gelling with the others and gradually participated in some physical activities. For the next three to four months, nothing unusual was noticed in her behaviour. However, gradually she started talking much more than normal and her unsolicited counselling monologues became a source of irritation to others. We also noticed that she had begun to talk incoherently.

Quite often, she would announce that she was certain Professor Goswami would be coming the following day to take her with him. We consulted the psychiatrist and he prescribed some medication. This did subdue her. But gradually, her appetite reduced. We noticed that she had started looking pale and had lost weight. She surely looked sick.

Then suddenly, one morning while climbing the three steps up to the main veranda, she fell like a fig falling from the mother tree. Such a fall would normally not cause any serious damage to an average human being, even if old.

Unfortunately, this was not so in her case. She complained of severe pain in her right leg and was unable to get up. She was taken to the hospital and an x-ray showed multiple fractures that required surgery. Admitted to the Guwahati Medical College hospital, she underwent surgery. The surgeon had to implant a metal strip to join the broken pieces of bones below her knee joint. A cast was put on her leg for forty-five days. After a couple of days, she was allowed to move short distances with the help of a walker. Back at Seneh, initially she looked bright and cheerful and to cap it all, seemed to have a healthy appetite.

Unfortunately, her sufferings did not end there. While walking with the support of the walker, she suddenly felt her bone had given way again. She was in great pain. An x-ray confirmed the worst, her bone had become so brittle, the implanted metallic support got disengaged and shattered her bones even further, as if they were glass.

She needed another operation and within days,

suffered another fracture, this time on the other leg. Now she was confined to the bed, writhing and complaining of pain all day long. The doctors said there was hardly any scope for further treatment and said that they could not alleviate her sufferings, except for taking recourse to palliative care. She was, in all probability, suffering from bone malignancy.

Like a fossilised piece of wood, she perforce got completely confined to the bed. With days, gradually, she became unable to move her torso or her limbs. But her mind got somehow sharper as if all her energy was now concentrated only on her brain and her tongue. She would deliver long sermons to the attending nurses and to others who came near her bed. Some of these sermons had substance and logic, while others delivered in her hoarse and inimical voice sounded like black gram roasted to burst on a bed of hot sand over the hearth. At such times, whatever she said was incoherent and, at times, abusive without reason.

I distinctly remember the morning when I approached her bed and placed my hand on her arm as a gesture of compassion. She literally pushed my hand away as if it was a wasp about to sting her and shouted, 'Leave me alone. It is you who conspired to ruin my life.' Such sudden outbursts were causes of irritation to others, as she would erupt like a volcano lashing out with her tongue. At other times, she was a picture of congeniality, coherence and coolness, displaying her scholarship abilities with a sound and distinctive mind.

Days passed. Our support staff worked overtime to feed and nurse her. Gradually, her mood swings became frequent. Her appetite diminished and she became pensive and moody. But alas! Despite our best efforts, bed sores appeared, first seemingly harmless oval-shaped bluish-black marks on the skin of her back and inner thighs. The sores started spreading day by day and enveloped the other areas of her body. Her complaints of pain and uneasiness increased.

Doctors prescribed some medicine for application. No effect. Someone suggested sunlight would help. We literally lifted her naked body, made her lie face down and exposed her sores to the sun for hours on end. All along, our dedicated nurses kept her cool with a hand fan and spread protective covers on the unaffected parts of her naked body. Unfortunately, this did not help either. Someone advised the application of coconut oil, camphor and the juice of neem leaves. We tried everything suggested by all and sundry, including tips posted on the internet. The sores kept increasing with each passing day. She writhed in pain and squirmed like a wounded bird. The frequency of her shrieks increased. Oh God! How heart-rending were those short, shrill cries!

The worst was still to come. And, when it did come, it came like a hawk swooping down upon its prey. The skin over the sores started peeling off, exposing raw, darkish flesh. The peeling increased every day. The most badly affected areas were her back, thighs and calves. As if that were not enough, to satisfy the evil designs of fate, the exposed flesh started decaying rapidly with a foul smell emanating from it. Within a month, almost two-thirds of her back and legs were affected. Even today when I think back about her sufferings my eyes moisten with compassion.

The days rolled by agonisingly. Roma's energy dissipated to the lowest level. She stopped complaining about her pains, her groans got feebler as if God had at last granted her mercy, showered her with special powers to withstand her pain and bestowed upon her the ability to quietly endure suffering. Occasionally, in her delirium, she would blurt out in a feeble but resolute voice, 'Look, Professor Goswami has come to take me. I told you, he will surely come.'

Finally, the light went off and the shimmer in her eyes dimmed forever. The nurses wailed. The other residents' faces got wet with tears. One could see panic in their eyes.

Roma's cremation was carried out as per Hindu tradition. Both the nurses did the honour of lighting the funeral pyre and conducted the other rituals.

Tulumai

Cheerful Despite Tragedies And Mishaps

Life was fun for young Tulumai. At eight, Tulu was the apple of her parents' eyes. Thin, tall and radiant, she remained calm even when she was required to go hungry or when defeated in a game of one-legged skip and jump (Kut Kut by name) that she played with her friends on a rectangular map of equal blocks in two rows drawn in their grassless courtyard. Occasionally, she would pull up her knee-length striped pyjamas to avoid them from slipping down as she jumped on the squares.

Little Tulu had only one frock which she would wear on special occasions. So invariably in summer, she was bare-bodied except the pyjama. In winter, she had an Eri (a thick local silk yarn famous for its strength and warmth) cloth tied around her neck. Another problem was her long hair that fell constantly over her eyes, obstructing her vision. According to the rules of the game, after the one-legged jumps to cross the blocks ended at the far end of the rectangle, the player could stand with both legs for a short while, before the return journey to base, once again on one leg. She would invariably take this momentary pause to push her hair away. Her soft-spoken nature, simplicity and honesty in playing the game made her popular with all the young girls of the locality. Most of them were school drop-outs. Tulu had dropped out of school when she was eight.

Her parents had no land of their own and tilled a portion of land belonging to a wealthy landlord. Landowners gave chunks of their land on lease to different villagers for farming. The lessees handed over 70 per cent of the produce to the owner and kept the rest for themselves. In those days, a single crop, usually paddy, was cultivated. Tulu's parents tilled a little over an acre of land for the landlord. Their share was enough to cater for a year's supply of grain to feed the nine hungry members of the family–Tulu's parents and six of her siblings. She was the third eldest.

They did not own a home, but lived in a small, thatch-roofed bamboo hut in one corner of the landlord's sprawling compound. To augment their income, the father also worked as a daily labourer on spare days.

Her mother wove garments like the *gamosa* (a scarf symbolic of the ethnic Assamese culture, worn by men on their shoulders), or cotton *chador* and *mekhela*, worn by women. Demand for her handloom products was scarce, because almost every household had a loom. The extra earnings by the parents catered for the other items necessary for subsistence. Her eleven-year-old elder sister was employed to look after the two-year-old grandson of the landlord. For her work, she earned a couple of rupees per month, meals and occasionally dresses. When she outgrew the dresses, Tulu inherited them.

When six, Tulu was enrolled in the local primary school. But her parents could not afford the books and notebooks. Immediately after each annual exam, she begged senior students to gift her their used books. There was a very high demand for these books as 50 per cent of the students could not afford new books. Tulu's genial nature and her attractive looks ensured that there were enough donors. Unfortunately, almost all the books were soiled and invariably had a few pages missing or torn.

She was good in studies. The lone teacher who taught all subjects to all the students of all classes was fond of her and gave her special attention. He also gave her chalk to write on the slate given to her by the landlady. She also occasionally gave her homemade sweets. Tulu always asked her for an extra sweet to take home to share with her younger siblings. When Tulu was ten, she completed her primary education. That also marked her exit from student life.

Two things stood in her way. First, the high school was far away. Second, the family could not afford the expense. Moreover, she was now supposed to begin earning and contribute to the family kitty.

Her adolescence was spent learning household jobs, doing needle work and working in the fields, harvesting the ripe paddy with the help of a sickle. She would collect the crop into small bundles and pile them together into a heap. Her father and elder brother would tie the small bundles together into larger ones that they then carried home, two at a time on their shoulders. The 7:3 division was done at this stage.

The menfolk then dried the bundles by spreading them in the courtyard. The grain was separated from their stalks by repeatedly driving a pair of bullocks over the. It was now the job of Tulumai and her mother to flip the grain up and down on a bamboo plate called *kula*. To separate the chaff from the grain. Tulumai was adept in two aspects of the farming process: she could plant saplings in neat rows on the marshy land, very quickly. She says all the villagers praised her lavishly, since she was only ten and could plant more saplings than grownups with thirty years of experience. Consequently, in addition to her work on the leased land, she was in demand to work in nearby fields. She earned a rupee for each 100 square metres, a good amount for her age. The money earned by her and her mother was used for buying clothes for the siblings.

By fifteen, Tulumai was also an expert weaver; her needlework was in demand although clientele was limited to the village. Much earlier, when she was merely eleven, Tulumai had to change her style of dressing. She was now forced to wear a frock or tie a piece of cloth over her body. By thirteen, she had graduated to a Mekhela, the ankle-length skirt and chadar and half-sleeved blouse worn by women of Assam. That is what she wears to this day. I can imagine what a petite and attractive young woman, Tulumai must have been when she was young. Even now at sixty-five, she looks calm and serene with twinkling eyes, even eyebrows, a long nose and an ever-existing grin.

She boasts she had very long silky hair, which she parted in the middle, made a braid and tied it up with red lace. Her skin was unblemished, smooth and light, wheatish-brown in colour. She and her mother wove the dresses she wore. She had three pairs of them, two simple ones in cotton with red borders woven with red cotton thread on a hand-operated loom. One metre normally takes around four hours to weave and the floral pattern takes ten times more time. Nevertheless, the rural womenfolk in this part of India still continue with the practice of weaving at home.

Her third dress was presented to her by an aunt. The *chadar* was of very fine cotton yarn and the *mekhela* woven out of the Pat silk yarn popular in this part of the country. The light cream-coloured yarn is known for its lustre and strength and if used properly can last a lifetime.

With her red-bordered *chadar*, red blouse and cream *mekhela* draped beautifully on her lithe body, Tulumai was considered the most beautiful girl in the village. 'But I was always reserved, withdrawn and a no-nonsense type. That kept the boys away,' said Tulumai.

At eighteen, Cupid struck. Dhaniram was a handsome man with his athletic build, piercing eyes and youthful gusto. He was the best player of the *dhol*, a local drum that is played by hanging it on the shoulders. It is played with a bamboo rod called *dholar mari* held in the right hand. Reverse is true for a southpaw. The left hand maintains the rhythm on the other face of the drum. The *dhol* is hit with real force with the *dholar mari*.

In Dhaniram's case, when he played the drum, his muscles bulged out, displaying his masculinity. Tulumai, on her part, was an adept Bihu dancer, the famous folk dance of the ethnic groups that inhabit the plains of the North East region. The dance is accompanied by the *dhol* and two percussion instruments, a flute made from the horn of a buffalo and a small cymbal peculiar to the area.

The two met at a cultural function to celebrate the Bihu harvest festival. They fell in love and their courtship continued for more than a year. In the interim, Tulumai lost her elder sister.

Her parents never approved of their courtship, mainly because nothing was known about Dhaniram's background. He lived alone in a nearby village and worked as a farm labourer. It was rumoured that he had some secret sources of income, since his lifestyle was somewhat opulent. To allay her fears, he told her that his parents had left behind a small fortune that he dipped into whenever he ran short of cash. He said he was an orphan with no siblings and hailed from a village far away. When orphaned, at eighteen, he left the village because his relatives were eying his inherited land, so he quickly sold it. He further claimed that he was asked to leave the village as the head there caught him alone with his widowed daughter in her room. He said that the older woman was using him but no one believed him.

Tulu, deeply in love, believed every word of his story. She eloped with him when she was twenty. She had to–she had missed her periods for two months and knew the import.

Their conjugal life initially was one of bliss and contentment. He worked hard and his stash of extra money helped add to his income. However, as the months and years passed, his true character came to light. He disappeared often, and soon Tulu discovered he was seeing another woman. To make matters worse, he became a habitual tippler. He would come back home late, completely drunk. He would then be abusive, and twice, he even beat her mercilessly.

She was angry and frustrated. She had abandoned her parents trusting him. Now, with two daughters to look after, and her own health, not as robust as it used to be, he became increasingly irresponsible and unfaithful. Initially, his drinking bouts were limited to two or three times a week but later, became a daily affair. She thought it was because they had used up the extra money he had, so she started augmenting their income by taking up work to plant rice seedlings for wealthy farmers. But it did not help.

In the meantime, her father expired after a short illness. One of her younger sisters, too, died within five months of her father's death. Tulu visited her family often, something she couldn't do when her father was alive, since he was really angry at her elopement and decided to abandon her.

Meanwhile, Dhaniram also took to gambling. He never bothered to ask how she was making both ends meet. Gradually his violence towards her also increased. Dhaniram had turned her life into hell.

Tulu can never forget the midnight knock on their door. Dhaniram was snoring beside her with their daughters sleeping in between. She opened the door to find a few policemen with guns standing there. Her husband woke up and tried to flee through the rear door, but he was apprehended.

Dhaniram was arraigned for robbery and murder that he purportedly committed earlier and was kept in prison as a non-bailable undertrial.

Tulu's life came to a grinding halt. She had no money. Also her health after the delivery of her second daughter was fragile. Her capacity for hard work had waned. She could not go out to work as her younger daughter was still an infant, and the older one was barely four years old. She could not earn enough to even feed them once a day. With the stigma attached to the family because of her husband, no one was willing to help.

Her widowed mother came to her rescue and took her home. The family was now living on an old-age pension of twenty rupees a month. All her siblings worked in different households but their combined earnings were just a little over fifty rupees per month. Tulu's eldest brother, probably the most capable of all, had migrated to another town and was living alone, working as a restaurant waiter. He was just about able to pay for his rent and could hardly help much.

Then, a few years later, one fateful rainy afternoon, her husband reappeared, completely sozzled. The police could not conclusively prove his complicity in the crime in a court of law. He was released.

He wanted to start life anew with her but Tulu would have none of it. She told him firmly that she will not pardon a man who had so ruthlessly betrayed her love and trust. She also told him that she knew about his crime as he had once bragged about it in a drunken stupor. With the help of her landlord, he was literally thrown out of the property. Later she heard that he was living with another woman. Within a few years, he died of liver disease. She never shed any tears for him.

When her youngest daughter was three years old, Tulu's mother arranged to send her to a destitute home and her daughters to a children's home run by the state's Social Welfare Department. Both these state homes were located at two remote corners of Guwahati. The city is 100-odd km away from their village.

Tulu stayed in the destitute home for more than five years. In this period, back home, tragedy struck the family repeatedly. First a younger sister, then a younger brother died of different ailments because timely medical help could not reach them. When these tragedies occurred, Tulu was permitted to go home for a short duration.

Life at the Destitute Home was lonely, but uneventful. The inmates spent their time gossiping and practising their hobbies. The food cooked by the portly cook was just enough for sustenance, but never good enough to satisfy the palate. Some of the women were quarrelsome, ever ready to pick up fights. A few used vulgar, filthy languages and unabashedly displayed their sexual frustration.

Tulu was always quiet and amiable and spent most

of her time alone, mostly engrossed in needlework. Her mild and pleasing manners endeared her to all, including the government officials in charge. The head of the officials, a portly gentleman, often summoned her home to help his wife in household chores. The lady was kind to her. In return for her services, Tulu earned a good meal and the various sewing kits required for her hand embroidery workpieces. The home sold her neat and attractive handiwork to visitors. Tulu looked forward for the summons from the headman. It meant a welcome break from the monotonous routine. The writer had the opportunity to meet one of the supervisors, now retired, who worked in the destitute home. She spoke highly of Tulu's nature and of her ability to endear herself to all. Tulu must have been and even today is a very soft-spoken genial person who does not talk ill of anyone and always maintains a low profile.

Tulu describes her days at the Destitute Home as uneventful. She despised the company of a few of her co-residents. She also felt abandoned and lonely though her younger brother came to meet her often. He brought news about the hardships and challenges the family was facing. He also kept track of the well-being of her children. But after her brother died, she hardly had any news from home or of the children, except twice, when she was allowed to go home for a day or two.

She stayed there for six years. In the seventh year,

she was informed about the illness of her old mother who was almost bed-ridden. With her younger sisters already married, the mother lived alone. Tulu requested the authorities for permission to go home for a year. It was denied. So she opted to leave the home for good and shifted to her mother's place. She worked hard to earn a living as a farm labourer. By that time, the landlord had reduced the quantum of leased land to them by half because there were no male farm hands in the family after her younger brother died.

For the land he allowed them to till, for the strenuous ploughing jobs, Tulu took the help of some of the village elders. The rest of the farming jobs she did herself. It was a tough call.

When her mother's health improved, Tulu left home to work as a knitting and embroidery instructor at a school more than 200 km from her mother's home. The owner of the institute had met Tulu at the Destitute Home and had been highly impressed by her work. The lady was happy to employ her. Tulu first went through a short training stint before she qualified to be a full-time Instructor. She worked there for more than two years. She was happy and contented.

Then her mother began to complain of loneliness and ill-health. Her elder daughter had to leave the children's home at the age of sixteen, as was the rule. To make matters worse, the vocational training school was unable to pay Tulu regularly because the new generation was not interested in embroidery. Tulu, therefore returned home along with her sixteen-year-old daughter.

A year later, financial hardships forced her to leave home and work in a cotton yarn factory. The factory was located on the other bank of the mighty Brahmaputra. Initially she commuted from home, crossing the river by ferry each day. This was easy in the dry season. But with the onset of the rainy season, the river became treacherous. It swelled and the banks became further apart. Every now and then, the ferry service got disrupted. It became impossible to commute from home.

Tulu took her daughter along to her place of work and hired a small hut. Every month, they went home for a couple of days to help the mother in whichever way they could. Later, her daughter also picked up a job in the same factory. But within a year, the factory had to down its shutters because of heavy losses. Fate had played truant with her again. Both of them had to come back to her mother's place.

The responsibility to make both ends meet fell on Tulu. It became a huge challenge. There were three mouths to feed. On top of it, her mother's health started deteriorating fast. She worked very hard to cater to their minimum needs.

Then another blow came her way. Her only surviving brother started having serious psychological issues owing to depression. Tulu sent her daughter to look after her brother. In about a year's time, the condition of her brother deteriorated. He lost his mental balance. Tulu had to bring both her brother and daughter back home. The poor man lived with them for two years, mostly loitering in the village and died thereafter, untreated for his mental maladies. Thus, one by one, her siblings died, falling like unripe mangoes from the mother tree due to strong unseasonal winds.

A year thereafter, her elder daughter, then seventeen, was married off to a man whom the girl met when she was with her uncle. The couple lived far away from her.

Tulumai was around fifty, lithe, supple and full of womanly grace. She was healthy and extremely hard-working. A widower in the village with no children, expressed a desire to take her home as his wife. He was ready to adopt her younger daughter, who was going to be sixteen shortly, as his own. Even the village elders, shedding tradition, approved of the match. But Tulu spurned his offer. Ultimately, the village elders decided to let her be, with a strange condition. She was to be married with all fanfare to the *Kirton Puthi*, a religious scripture. The *Kirton*, a book of verses eulogising the life of Lord Krishna written by the most revered saint of Assam, the Vaishnavite reformist and cultural wizard, Srimonto Sankara Deva, is worshipped as a scripture of God and occupies pride of place in the altar of the 'Namghar', a place of worship and devotional community singing. She accepted their condition.

Strangely, the marriage of the widow with the scripture did take place, in elaborate ritualistic manner, with all funfare. I never knew such a practice existed and honestly, disbelieved this part of her story. I tried to check if this practice is prevalent in some societies in rural Assam, but I drew a blank. Recently, a learned lady confirmed the practice does exist. The marriage is solemnised with all fanfare like a normal marriage in some rural societies of central Assam.

After the strange marriage, Tulu decided, it was time to get her younger daughter home. The girl regularly went to school from the Children's Home, and had even appeared in the High School exam but failed. After coming to live with them, the girl started troubling Tulu. She bickered, she was lonely and missed the food served at the Children's Home. Tulu and her mother were bewildered. The daughter refused to help them in any household chores and was not ready to go out to work either. At the earliest opportunity, Tulu and her mother got her married to a young man from a nearby village. The couple were happy, but within a year, the girl died of complications during childbirth.

Finally, Tulu and her ailing mother were alone in the village. Tulu had to earn for both. The village headman helped her to receive old-age pension from the government. The mother-daughter duo thus received Rs 600 a month. She continued working as a farm hand.

Life continued, every day a challenge. She toiled hard without rest. The medication was costly. Finally in the year 2008, her mother passed away. Tulu was left truly alone. The house was in a sad state of disrepair. Gradually, her capacity for hard work waned. But Tulu kept fighting all odds to survive. Her elder daughter never even came to visit. Her two surviving sisters were struggling to manage their own families. Her youngest sister, who was married to a music teacher in a small town, was in touch regularly but with five mouths to feed, she could not help financially.

By 2016, the hut was no longer liveable. The old cast iron sheets on the roof got completely corroded. The roof leaked profusely. The walls withered. The landlord refused to get it repaired. He wanted her to vacate the place. He used different pressure tactics to scare her off the property. She was helpless. The village ignored her plight. Finally, she was given an ultimatum to vacate in three days or face physical eviction. She was sick, with a huge tumour on her right cheek which was extremely painful. And had nowhere to go.

A local TV channel got wind of her plight and aired a video about her. Financial help poured in from compassionate viewers. The authorities of a Home for the aged came and took her with them. But she did not like it there. She became morose and withdrawn. She pestered her younger sister to take her away. This lady finally approached Seneh. We were a little reluctant and rang up the NGO where she had been living. They told us that Tulu was very reclusive and was having trouble adjusting to their surroundings.

We asked Tulu to describe her problems. She looked pitiable with her tumour on the left cheek, which was now the size of a tennis ball. We decided to accommodate her right away. The very next morning, she was taken to the hospital and admitted there. Next day, after the mandatory blood tests, her tumour was surgically removed. The surgeon said that it was full of pus. It must have pained her a lot.

Two days later, Tulu came back with a bandage and a large grin on her face. She was finally free from the pain. It was a reassuring sight. From that day on, Tulu has been living with the others like a family member, her amiable, amenable and mild nature endearing her to everyone.

She is now an integral part of the Seneh family. She has an interesting husky voice, and it appears, the words come out of her throat with the lips and tongue working as second fiddles. Thanks to the contributions of the public after the telecast written about earlier, there is plenty of money in her bank account. We wanted to hand over the bank papers to her sister since Tulu will not need the money so long as she stays with us. But the sister refused.

Her money is still there in her account untouched. The only time she requested for a small withdrawal was to pay for a meal for poor cancer patients and their attendants at a local cancer hospital. It was a revelation for us.

Since then, every week, on Saturdays, we distribute free lunches to approximately 150 people in the cancer hospital. Our members and volunteers contribute, by turn, to meet the expenses.

Tulu's embroidery and knitting products are considered the best that the residents of Seneh make. They are the works of a master.

Tulu today, with her suave manners and elegant looks, is the undisputed darling of all visitors who come to Seneh every now and then.

Purnima Rabha

A Miraculous Turnaround

Purnima's life is probably the most fascinating anyone will ever come across. It is a life full of contradictions and tribulations, good and evil, struggle and defeat, valour and cowardice, and above all, of providence and luck. She is endowed with an iron will to face all adversities with calm and élan; her never-say-die attitude has made her what she is today.

Honestly, I am unable to decide how to start depicting her life story. Therefore, let me begin with Purnima as she is today. If the reader ever visits Seneh, a middle-aged, scrawny woman in her fifties will probably greet him or her with folded hands, a shy smile on her face. And what a face it is! It exudes a singular radiance.

Her jet-black lustrous hair curls down in waves like the ripples on the surface of a lake, caused by the gentle wind.

Another striking feature is her unblemished light brown skin and natural eyebrows comparable to the shape of the third night's moon. Immediately below are her bright oscillating eyes, and a large, pointed nose. In totality, it is a very pleasant face with prominent dimples. Her steps are measured and the gait reserved and calm. She hardly talks and prefers working silently or quietly reading a book in a corner. But she participates wholeheartedly in all group activities and displays rapt devotion during community prayers that are offered twice a day.

She has a slim, strong yet shapely body, her waist so small that it can be encircled by the palms of two large hands. She has an attractive and serene look about her. No one will believe that she has a grown-up granddaughter of marriageable age or that she was born in 1969.

She has exemplary culinary skills and dances with the grace of a swan, especially the Assamese folk dance *Bihu*. She is an avid reader of Assamese books, the only language she knows, and I was thrilled to learn that she is able to write well. I had asked her to write about her life, and what a fascinating story she penned! I added whatever other information I gathered from her acquaintances and her TB-afflicted brother who lives nearby.

This is how the story of her fascinating, eventful life unfolded before me.

I remember distinctly that winter evening when I was in Delhi devouring a Frederic Forsyth, when I got a call from the amazingly dedicated and compassionate Jutika, Seneh's Chief Coordinator and Head Caretaker. She said that someone rang up to inform her about a dying woman lying on the corner of a street intersection not very far from Seneh. She asked my permission to go and help. Granted, she rushed to the spot and what she saw and narrated was appalling and dreary, if not ghastly.

There was this woman lying on the pavement barely breathing, except for a few laboured gasping breaths at irregular intervals. Both her legs were injured and swollen as if they were an elephant's legs, with foul-smelling liquid oozing out of them. Maggots and lice were seen crawling out from the wounds. Her face was swollen, lips parched, the skull covered in small patches of hair, the rest fallen off in clusters. The eyelids were so swollen that there was no way to know if the eyes were intact.

Jutika learnt the woman had been lying there for the past four to five days. Although, it was a busy intersection, and hundreds passed by, no one had bothered to help her. People, in fact, took a detour to avoid the living dead.

Immediately after she was brought to Seneh, the woman was taken to a local private hospital with close links to us in an ambulance. She was given oxygen support in the vehicle. The Sun Valley Hospital in Guwahati has been providing yeomen service to the residents of Seneh by giving free treatment for the last two years. Jutika first asked help from the head of the hospital, who not only despatched the ambulance but was himself waiting outside to receive the patient.

Without any delay, the doctors admitted her to the Intensive Care Unit and put her on a ventilator. The attending doctors opined that the prognosis was bleak and she may not survive the night. Her BP was very low and her pulse, feeble. A blood test indicated onset of multi-organ failures.

Luckily, next afternoon, she started breathing regularly. Her blood pressure stabilised. She opened her eyes. The continuous medicated drips given under the loving care of the nurses under the hawk eyes of the doctors had brought the woman back to life. The doctors later said they considered it a miracle and will of God that she lived. Probably, if our dedicated and extremely compassionate team were a tad late in responding to her sufferings, she would not have survived.

Thus, thanks to providence, Purnima got a new life. In ten days, she was discharged from hospital, although her wounds had not healed. Our nursing team thereafter took over, treating her wounds with regular cleaning and dressing and administering her antibiotics. In a month's time, Purnima was able to move around in a laboured fashion, supported by a walker, without help.

Her recovery was gradual but extremely promising.

She was taken to the hospital every two weeks for review. The doctor's guidance and the care she received from the team at Seneh seemed to have saved her. But alas, in the process, the medics found another ailment that could end her life at any moment. Her heart had three leaking valves.

We took her to another private hospital known for its cardiology department. The head of the department, a super specialist, is well known in South East Asia. A large number of patients flock to him from all over the world for consultations. I personally took her to him and explained how our team had saved her life. He was mighty impressed by the humanitarian work at Seneh. He not only examined her thoroughly, but also decided to be personally present when her electrocardiogram was being conducted, all without any charge. He came out of the ECG lab with a concerned, worried look. I instantly understood that there was something very wrong with Purnima. Later, the doctor confirmed the findings of the earlier hospital and explained her condition in graphic detail.

When I asked him pointedly if a valve replacement surgery will save her, he said, her heart is beyond any surgical intervention. He prescribed medication and advised that she be confined to bed as much as possible. He said that such patients do not survive more than six months. He advised a second visit after a month.

Accordingly, when she went to the doctor after a month, he was astonished to find that her condition had certainly improved. After a year's intensive medications and regular check-ups including ECGs, the doctor rang me up, his voice full of excitement, informing me that Purnima had recovered completely. He said, he never believed in miracles, but seeing Purnima's recovery, he could only say that miracles do happen.

Thus, Purnima survived two major threats to her life. On an earlier occasion also, she had come back from the brink of death. At the tender age of eight, she had sustained second-degree burns. With home medication for a week, the injuries had worsened and she was on the brink of death. She was finally admitted to the local Medical College hospital in the burns ward. In a fortnight, her wounds had healed, astonishing the doctors. Except for a few permanent burn marks on her body, she was able to resume normal life, running and playing with other children of her age.

Today, Purnima with her captivating smile is a bundle of energy, looking content and cool. The time has now come to give the reader a peep into her eventful, fascinating and probably, romantic past. In a way, perhaps she is lucky to have lived a life of strife and contradictions, of love and despair, of valour and surrender, and above all, a life of miracles.

Let me start from the beginning.

***

He was a strong man, his biceps hard as stone, his chest muscles firm, dense and compressed. He pulled the hand cart every day, from morning till late evening, laden with different merchandise of the merchants. His legs were equally firm, the calf muscles rock solid. He took measured and cautious steps, taking care not to slip, specially while pulling his heavily loaded cart on wet roads. A slip meant inviting disaster.

He missed his wife and two young toddlers back home in a remote village in the hinterland of Bihar. He managed to visit them just once in two years. He longed for their company.

She was twenty, vivacious and radiant and worked in her mother's country liquor vend, on the foothills of Narakasur, a low hill surrounded by thick vegetation in Guwahati. One side of the hill is covered with lush green teak trees covering three hectares of land. The trees had been planted four years back, in neat rows, by the state's social forestry department.

Their vend was tucked away inside thick tropical shrubs. A lonely dirt road lined with trees of different sizes and thick vegetation connected it to the main road. The place was supposedly safe from the hawk eyes of the state's Excise Department. Once a Sub-Inspector did pay a surprise visit. Thereafter, it meant regularly greasing his palms. Her mother made the heady brew at home. In addition, they also sold fried and boiled black gram garnished with onion and green chillies, as a snack. The liquor shop was a refuge for daily workers, cart and rickshaw pullers, drivers, washermen and the like, all poorly paid and employed in physical, backbreaking jobs. Business was lukewarm in the daylight hours, but in the evenings, the place buzzed, with a dozen or so customers crowding in the small, kerosene lamp-lit hut, with its rickety wooden benches and tables. Her maternal uncle, a muscular man with a no-nonsense tough look, worked as the bouncer.

Purnima's father, the cart puller, healthy and energetic, was not a frequent visitor to her mother's kiosk. He visited it only when he was exhausted. With iron resolve, he would restrict himself to just one glass on such occasions. Thereafter, he would retire to his one-room cottage and begin preparing his dinner of half a dozen thick *rotis,* which he devoured with crushed onion, chillies and salt as accompaniment. He hardly talked, but after a drink, would often hum a folk tune in his native Bhojpuri. His interaction with others was rare. His manner was always mild, endearing and civilised.

Purnima's mother developed a liking for him. This liking blossomed into love. She threw aside all social and ethnic barriers, like one tramples dry leaves in the fall season. One fine evening, she went over to his hut, knowing fully well that he was married and had two children back home. It was of no consequence to her. He accepted her, and they lived thereafter as husband and wife, totally devoted to each other.

He sired seven children, three boys and four girls, from this union, in a span of eleven years. Purnima was the third eldest. 'I have seen my younger two brothers sucking my mother's breasts simultaneously', recalled Purnima, in her matter-of-fact memoir. 'Because of my mild manners and quiet demeanour, I was the apple of my dad's eyes. We had a bonding that the other siblings envied,' she wrote.

Endowed with robust health, and an ability to work hard without rest, her father also paddled a cycle rikshaw in the evening hours, ferrying passengers around till midnight. He required money to support two families, one at Guwahati with nine members and the other at Bihar with three members.

Money was always scarce. Purnima, therefore, grew up in hardship and poverty and learnt early in life how to conquer pangs of hunger and the pain of deprivation.

Eight-year-old Purnima was in Class II, in a local school, when her mother once again decided to start her ancestral business of brewing and selling rice beer in their old kiosk. Purnima's youngest brother, Arjun, was only nine months old. The mother entrusted the household jobs and the care of the nine-month-old to Purnima and her elder sister. Six months later, however, the eldest sister eloped with a Muslim youth, leaving Purnima to manage house and baby.

'I was very fond of Arjun. We developed a mother-son-like bonding from the day I began looking after him,' wrote Purnima. She added: 'I took on this responsibility when I was only eight, and was forced to give up regular classes. Whenever I could manage the time, I went to school. My teachers admonished me for my absence, but they also knew about our domestic situation, so they let me be. As for me, whenever Arjun slept, I opened my books and did my homework. One of my classmates, a boy who lived in the neighbourhood kept me up-to-date with the daily progress of lessons in the class, and the homework.'

It was a challenging task for an eight-year-old to take on the responsibility of looking after an infant. She wrote in her clean, but not-so-correct hand for me to read. 'He troubled me a lot, especially when he was hungry. He would cry non-stop. I would take him in my arms and go running the one-odd kilometre distance to the kiosk for his feed. The dirt track to the kiosk was scary, zigzagging through wild, dense vegetation, interspersed with huge trees. Monkeys jumped around, scaring the life out of me. Clutching my brother to my chest, I used to dash as fast as I could go. To avoid the deadliest patch, I normally took a short route that waded through a marshy shoal, infested with leeches. Often, the leeches clawed on my bare legs, mainly between the toes, sucking my blood.

Usually, it was my mother who noticed the blood and she would pull the slimy creatures away with difficulty.'

'We had an aunt who lived nearby with her baby. One day it was raining heavily and I could not take my brother to my mother for his regular feed. Arjun kept crying uncontrollably. My sister made him some thin lentil soup, but he refused to drink it. Then she tried to give him sweet rice water, but Arjun would have none of it. He was very restless. Desperate, I ran to my lactating aunt and begged her to offer her breast milk to our baby brother. She refused, then yelled at me, asking how dare I make such an absurd request. It was the last time I ever spoke to her, although she lived long. How can a mother be so cruel? That question still disturbs me.'

For one entire year, she could hardly attend school. Her brother clung to her. He was also constantly sick. On lean days, her mother stayed home, closing her shop till the evenings so that Purnima could attend school. 'My teachers were angry, but because I was the best student in my class, they were patient with me,' wrote Purnima. Then she suffered the burn from the kerosene stove that I wrote about earlier.

Finally, her brother began playing happily with the others around their home. Purnima could now afford to be reasonably regular at school. Arjun was an extremely weak child and was often sick. He clung to her when ill, disrupting her studies.

Once, he was admitted to the Guwahati Medical College hospital for seven days. 'I stayed with him in the ward sharing the food given to him by the hospital without proper sleep. In the morning, my mother or sister came to relieve me for a few hours so that I could trek back home through the hillocks, take a bath, freshen up and return after a light meal.' Thus, the brother-sister duo developed a bonding that continues even today. He visits her at Seneh, although he has had three relapses of tuberculosis. He is around fifty, all skin and bones. We have been dissuading him from visiting her, keeping the interests of the old residents in mind.

She was finally regular at school by the time she was ten. Unfortunately, because of the disruptions in her studies, she was unable to top the class unlike previous years. By fourteen, she was a charming, suave young maiden with her Mongoloid-type slit eyes, curly jet black hair, measured grace and reserved manners. 'I came third in the annual examinations in class eight,' she lamented.

***

He was handsome in his own peculiar way, athletically built with wide shoulders, neatly brushed oiled hair, a thin moustache, and a few spiky bristles on his chin, like antennae on the roof of a car. Amit was a macho man. Every morning, when she walked to school, he was around, puffing a cigarette and blowing out the smoke from his nostrils. Suddenly, she became conscious of his hot stares on her face, chest and her long legs. She found herself reciprocating. He started waiting for her at a point, and then walk with her till the school was in sight. Then, he would leave, as they were careful not to be seen together by her other classmates, especially the teachers.

She told no one, except two of her close classmates, who vowed never to betray her confidence. Their relationship mushroomed like ferns and moss in the rainy season. Twice, she skipped school and went to a secluded place atop a hill, where Amit romanced her. On the second clandestine sojourn, he embraced and kissed her, then proposed. She was only fifteen, so she said that he would have to approach her mother with his proposal. In her naivety, she never asked him for his antecedents. Her mother did. Satisfied, she agreed. Her two elder daughters had eloped, so she did not think it wise to refuse.

Was it the start of the tragicomedy of her life? The answer is both 'Yes' and 'No'. The whimsical decisions of the Almighty are beyond our understanding or comprehension. They have no logic of jurisprudence, neither can they be challenged or questioned, but must be accepted as fate. The very words, *fait accompli*, are flawed, untenable. We mortal beings cannot question

Him, and we cannot ever ask why the oppressed and the poor are the victims of His wrath; these are beyond any rudimentary rule of law of equality as understood by us.

Coming back to Purnima's story, she tells me that her father was a very humble man, extremely hard-working, honest to the core, simple and amiable. He needed companionship and someone to comfort him after a day's hard work. Since his first wife was away, with her consent, he married the second one, Purnima's mother. 'I remember only once my father overstayed at Bihar and did not return for three months. We kept sending urgent messages asking him to return, but he did not come back. My mother was hysterical and we thought he had abandoned us. Then I suffered serious burn injuries and was hospitalised. When the news reached my father, he did not wait. He came back standing in an unreserved coach on the train and reached Guwahati; he came straight to the hospital from the railway station. The joy of meeting my father was the best medicine I could get. Within days, my injuries started healing,' wrote Purnima.

Her marriage was solemnised in a traditional manner, and she lived separately with her chauffeur-husband in a one-room rented accommodation not far from her mother's house. Purnima wanted to attend school, but her husband's timings did not suit her schedule, so she decided to pursue studies at home, taking advantage of a kind and dedicated teacher who lived nearby. The school agreed to allow her to appear in the matriculation examination as an absentee student.

'As husband and wife, we had perfect synergy and understanding. Our requirements were few. A portion of the money my husband earned, went to his widowed mother and elder sister, who lived together in their ancestral village. To cut on our expenditure, my husband even gave up smoking at my insistence, although, honestly, I adored the way he smoked leisurely. It gave him a macho look,' wrote Purnima. This is not exactly what she had written, but I have captured the gist.

Things started souring when her mother-in-law came to stay with them for a few days. But she did not go back as per plan. Soon, she started finding fault with Purnima over trivialities, such as the way she walked, dressed, or the time she spent on her books. Purnima was perturbed, but she never betrayed her feelings to her husband lest he tick off his mother.

In her own family, tragedies struck like a tsunami, ravaging not only the coast line but also its fringes. First, her brother Arjun was diagnosed with tuberculosis and admitted to the local TB hospital for six months. Next, one of her elder brothers was arraigned in an assault case, even though he insisted that he was innocent.

Then came the most fatal blow to the family that was like a bolt from the blue. One of her widowed maternal uncles, who lived nearby, was found dead in his house.

No one knew when he died. His corpse was discovered only when the neighbours complained about a foul smell. It created a commotion in their tribal community as they believed that if a body decays, the spirit turns into a ghost who starts residing in the corpse. They believed that if his safe abode is burnt, the ghost is infuriated and curses with evil consequences those who take part in the cremation. Hence there was nobody ready to carry the body to the funeral pyre.

Purnima's father found this belief absurd. He decided to call a few of his friends for help. As he hurried to call his friends, he was hit by a moving truck and died. As a consequence, not one but two corpses had to be carried to the cremation ground. A double tragedy.

These unhappy circumstances carried away the anchor of her life. From that time on, the ship of her life was tossed and thrown around with a vengeance that ultimately almost sank it.

Purnima conceived. On the advice of her mother-in-law, it was decided that she go to their village for the delivery. Amit promised to send money every month. He advised her to keep a small portion of the remittances for herself, and hand over the rest to her mother-in-law. However, the mother-in-law, instigated by her widowed daughter, resented the arrangement. First, she was upset that the money came to Purnima instead of her. Second, she did not see any reason for Purnima keeping anything aside. Hence she had to hand over the full remittances to her mother-in-law.

I did not want to get into any arguments for the sake of the child in my womb. So, I did not keep any money in hand. I resolved to tackle this after the delivery,' Purnima wrote.

In due course, a midwife helped her deliver a healthy girl. She also regularly massaged both the baby and the new mother. At the end of the month, when the midwife wanted her payments, the mother-in-law refused to give her any money. Purnima pawned an earring to pay the midwife.

When the baby was two months old, her husband came from Guwahati for the first time after the delivery. Purnima was overjoyed. He stayed back for a month spending all his time with the baby or loafing around the village. But, when after a month also, he did not talk of returning back to join his job, Purnima became suspicious. On probing, she found that he actually came back because he lost his job.

He, therefore, stayed back, helping his mother in farming and quarrelling with his widowed sister on flimsy grounds. The cool, even-headed Purnima always brokered peace. A year thereafter, he left for a faraway town with a friend.

For some months, there was no news from him. He did not send any money either. The mother-in-law, fuelled by the sinister designs of her sister-in-law, started suspecting that her son was sending Purnima money clandestinely.

As a result, plenty of verbal abuses came Purnima's way. With passing days, the abuses culminated in beatings. To add to her miseries, she was pregnant again. She decided to go back to her mother. But the mother-in-law refused to part with Purnima's first child. She was forced to go alone.

When she returned to her mother, she became the subject of debate and ridicule of her neighbours and relatives. They assumed her husband had driven her out.

A couple of months thereafter, she delivered a baby girl. When her husband learnt about it, he came running, leaving his job. He picked up a job as a garbage truck driver in Guwahati. They rented a house and once again started living happily together. Purnima's heart pained for the elder daughter. She missed her. But the mother-in-law never allowed the child to join her parents. Her husband advised her to have patience.

When the baby was three months old, her mother-in-law came visiting and insisted that Purnima go back with her. Her husband agreed. So reluctantly, she had to accompany her mother-in-law. Once back in the village, the same story repeated, like a stuck gramophone record.

The two widowed women often drank home-made rice beer together. When drunk, they hurled volleys of abuses at Purnima. In their society, brewing and drinking rice beer by both the sexes was common.

Amit, her husband, was always deceptive and unpredictable–much like the London weather. When he was at home, he was the perfect husband, loving and caring, but when away with his friends, he would forget about his family, wife and children. Then suddenly, he would resurface, only to play the perfect family man again.

Amit came back after four months.

Purnima finally complained about the harrowing treatment she was getting. He listened to both sides, brokered peace, and restored relative quiet. Then, one day his drunk mother picked up a fight with Purnima and in her mad rage, hit her hard on her back with a tree branch, inflicting injuries. Purnima was confined to bed for the next three days. Amit decided enough was enough. With his brother, he erected a mud hut nearby for Purnima and her daughters to stay separately. The mother once again refused to part with the elder daughter.

Amit went off after a couple of months and picked up a new job. Two months thereafter, he started sending money to Purnima that he asked her to share with his mother. Again, money became the bone of contention. The mother felt Purnima was not telling the truth about the sum she was receiving.

Matters came to a boil when, after a few months, Amit stopped sending money. 'I heard, he had started gambling and losing money. He also took to drinking. I began to doubt his fidelity as well. I heard rumours about his amorous activities,' wrote Purnima.

With no money or source of income, Purnima was like a fish out of water. She decided to go back to Guwahati and asked one of Amit's uncles for help. The podgy gentleman was extremely understanding and advised her against leaving. She stayed put.

Purnima decided to work to earn her living but the only work available in the remote village was farming, something she knew nothing about. Amit's aunt tenderly took Purnima under her wings and taught her the nuances of planting and harvesting paddy, the only crop the villagers cultivated. After a season's training, Purnima, the efficient farm labourer was born.

'The uncle and aunt were my saviours, my guardians and my altar of worship,' wrote Purnima. 'Life was tough but peaceful. In the non-agricultural season, I worked as a help in Amit's uncle's house and received enough to sustain myself with foodgrains, cereals, pulses and occasionally fish whenever they caught them from their pond.'

'Amit would surface occasionally, be his genial self, stay, roam, hug, laugh and leave as suddenly as he appeared, leaving some money in my hands. Every time he came, he brought presents, normally a sari for me and frocks for the daughters. Those were the most idyllic days of my life,' she wrote.

Unfortunately, her peace and tranquillity caused her sister-in-law to become envious. Quite often, the spiteful lady sneaked into her hut and destroyed whatever looked attractive, and also literally spoilt the broth by sprinkling excessive salt or chili powder on the food that Purnima cooked before departing for work. Once she even caught her own eldest daughter sneaking in and sprinkling sand on her cooked rice. Purnima thrashed her and subsequently shed buckets of tears. A fight broke out and Purnima was mercilessly beaten. She received serious injuries to her legs. The neighbours came and separated them.

Purnima went back to work on the farm. The injured leg troubled her, but her youth, robust health and iron will prevailed. Hearing about the upheaval from some sources, her husband came and advised Purnima to leave for Guwahati. Amit was then working at a brick kiln 100-odd km from Guwahati, carting bricks on the owner's dilapidated truck. He lived in a camp with others by the side of the kiln.

She left the village with her younger daughter. On his mother's insistence, Amit agreed to leave behind his eldest daughter. It was a decision Purnima regrets, even today. It was the final nail in the coffin of the mother-daughter relationship.

She hired a room near her mother's home, admitted her child to the local school and began working as a part-time maid. Within a year, the most devastating blow to her life fell on her head like a ton of bricks. In actuality, tons of bricks literally fell on Amit's head when the truck's helper unknowingly opened the side panel of the truck laden with bricks. Amit was dozing on the side of the truck. He succumbed to his injuries on way to the hospital.

Purnima was six months pregnant. His friends took Amit's body to his ancestral village for the last rites. Purnima went, too. His friends contributed generously to perform the rituals, including a feast on the thirteenth day of his demise for the entire village. 'Amit's brother took the lead and I suspect he used the balance for constructing a house for himself,' wrote Purnima. This statement from her positively ruffled me. Was it the lure of money that ruined her life?

Purnima thereafter returned to Guwahati, carrying with her the full burden of looking after her children without support.

In spite of her advanced pregnancy and health complications, she worked hard in four houses to earn money. Three months later, she delivered a male child. Her mother and sister helped, but there were whispers that her husband did not father the child. The boy did not survive long to carry the stigma of these rumours. He died on his fifteenth day of life. The whispers also died down.

It took her a week from the infant's demise to recover from the shock. Then she prepared herself to face the harsh realities of life. In addition to the four houses she worked in, she took up a part-time job of looking after a toddler in the evening hours. The parents of the child worked until late evenings. Purnima normally left her daughter with her sister when she was away for work, especially in the evenings. But, if the sister was unavailable, she took her daughter along. The arrangement worked well for a year. One day, the owners came back early to find Purnima's daughter on the floor by the side of their bed. She had dozed off with her head on the bed. This infuriated them. Purnima was fired.

She decided she needed more money to live comfortably with respect. She nurtured a brilliant idea. She started brewing liquor. Within days, her business grew and experienced drinkers opined that she made the best brew in the neighbourhood. With her flourishing business, she had enough money for all needs. She could even save. 'I wanted to buy a small plot of land and construct a hut. I also wanted my eldest daughter back. Accompanied by some elders, I went to the village to fetch her. But my mother-in-law hid her somewhere and stubbornly denied her existence. We came back empty-handed. The incident broke my heart into pieces,' wrote Purnima.

She continued the bootlegging business with more resolution. She had a dream. She would work harder for the sake of the daughter. She secretly vowed she will make her daughter the first graduate in the family. The daughter was good in studies. Purnima hired a home tutor to help her excel. The girl's academic records improved. She was the undisputed topper. She also excelled in extra-curricular activities. The ten-year-old was also a big help in looking after the house in her absence. She always cooked the dinner.

Purnima was one of the youngest bootleggers in town, petite and graceful. In addition, her single status attracted many men. She was smart enough to ward off their advances without it affecting her business. With her earnings, she bought a small plot of land, constructed a tin roofed mud house, bought a colour TV and some furniture. Everything looked bright and sunny for her.

Then, in a flash, all her dreams were destroyed.

One of her envious relatives informed the state Excise Department about her clandestine business. They raided her premises and closed it. She had to give a hefty sum as bribe to avoid an arrest. With her business shut, she felt as if the sky had fallen on her head, making her dizzy. She lost her sense of direction.

First, the colour TV was sold off. The next to go was the home tutor. Even the plastic chairs could not be saved. Purnima was in desperate need of money. She started to work as a sales help in a shop. She had to work from nine to nine, but the salary was inadequate. A road was being laid nearby and she realised that even labourers who earned Rs 250 per day were better off. The job was back-breaking, but she took it up. Her back and arms pained because she now carried heavy loads. After the day's hard work, she had no energy to cook or even wash her own dishes. The daughter took care of that. Purnima looked intently at the girl with pride and hope. She was fourteen, pretty, hardworking and intelligent, and very caring, and excelled in her studies as well.

One day, the girl eloped with a young businessman. Purnima never even bothered to find out if she was alive or well. Their umbilical cord was severed for good.

Then, in quick succession, two tragedies befell her. Her elder sister who was married and had three children died of tuberculosis. Then, her mother, another pillar of support for her, died after a brief illness. The burden of organising the last rites and subsequent rituals fell on her shoulders. She had to sell off her dwelling unit to meet the expenses. The only surviving members of her family were now Purnima, her TB-infected weak and sick younger brother, and the outcast sister who had married a Muslim.

An elderly, portly, bearded, soft-spoken Muslim mason, who lived with his wife and four children, not very far from her ancestral home employed her to mix the cement-sand mortar mixture as he laid brick walls. She would carry the mixture on her head in a *tasla* and bring it over to him. The mixture was smeared on every row and between the bricks to bind them together as he laid the wall. She then had to sprinkle water on the recently completed layers of brick walls, a process in construction to make the wall firm. She earned a daily wage of Rs 300–just enough to live comfortably and repay some of her debt as well as help her brother who was constantly sick.

The relationship between her and the mason soon grew thick. They shared their lunch boxes. Purnima often cooked mutton, his favourite dish and carried it along to share with him. They cycled to and fro to work together, she riding on the pillion. She often had dinner together with his family. She even fasted with him in the Ramadan month! Their bonhomie raised many an eyebrow. Was their relationship strictly professional? Her own relatives believe their relationship was flawed. She, however, denies this.

Meanwhile, the whispers about their relationship became louder, till the elders of their clan stepped in with their diktat. She was given two choices. Either she leave the neighbourhood and sever all relations with him or leave her job and retreat to her husband's village. She was thrown between the devil and the deep sea. She decided to vacate her ancestral place, and continued working with her saviour, the mason. She hired a shack to stay. But the rumours reached the family of the mason and he was forced to sack her.

Once again, the doe was alone, surrounded on all sides by barking dogs. To make matters worse, an old painful abscess on her leg which tormented her a couple of years ago, erupted. Within days, a second eruption occurred. The pain was excruciating and she was admitted to a government hospital.

As a rule, all in-patients in the hospital must have a personal attendant. Also, most of the medicines had to be purchased from the local market. Her brother could not help as he was too sick. She had no money to buy the medicines, so she was sent back home. She went back to her shack, but the owner had already leased it to someone else. Purnima was now limping in excruciating pain. She started sitting on the street corner and begged. Whatever she earned, she spent on buying a meal in the evening. In addition, she had to pay a rupee each day to sleep in the veranda of a nearby shop.

Her legs got steadily worse, they started swelling like balloons. Watery liquid started oozing out emanating a foul, acrid smell. The smell attracted flies. Ultimately, she was unable to move, unable to stand. She lay there on the street corner. Some people threw coins from a distance or left food packets near her. Finally, her wounds were so infected that maggots grew on both her legs. She could not even attend the call of nature. The foul smell from her decayed legs and the smell of her excreta combined was so repellent that passers-by would walk past with a cloth over their noses. Some took a detour to avoid her.

Finally, she collapsed, stopped feeling pain, hunger

or thirst. She became completely oblivious of her surroundings. Her urge to live evaporated. Then, as if by Providence, our intervention started....

Swapna

Forced To Marry Her Rapist

Swapna's perpetual pout, and her youthful exuberance were robbed permanently the day she was lured, abducted, kept hostage and violated by her self-proclaimed paramour, the village bad boy, 36 years ago. That day, the ebullient, energetic, doe-like sixteen-year-old, turned into a fossil of her former self. Before this abduction, she was the most attractive yet productive daughter of the village. Her polite demeanour, supple and nimble movements, lithe body ensured her selection to represent the village folk dance group that participated in the inter-village folk dance competitions organised at Bijni, the nearest town. This, combined with her mastery on the loom, and performance in studies, made her the darling of the village.

After her abduction, the two were traced and brought back to the village. Her desperate mother approached the village Panchayat for redressal. A meeting of the village elders was held to decide on a course of action. When Swapna and her abductor were summoned to the meeting, the boy's father begged for forgiveness. Swapna could not answer questions by the Panchayat members, but torrents of tears flowed down her cheeks, choking her. She had lost her ability to look straight into others' eyes for good. On the other hand, the boy, vocal but submissive, admitted his fault without any hesitation. He offered to take Swapna as his wife and look after her like a responsible husband.

After levying a hefty fine on him, the Panchayat elders decided in favour of his request. No one asked Swapna for her opinion. Even if they had, in all probability, Swapna would not have spoken, for she had lost her ability to decide or judge right from wrong. The trauma had sapped her spirit, her will, her determination—and worst of all, it had killed her hopes and aspirations, for ever. The Panchayat seemed oblivious to Swapna's condition.

Their judgement, in effect, meant forgiving him for his horrendous deeds. Such judgements are not uncommon in rural India. Even some learned judges of the Indian courts pronounce such judgements on the helpless victims of sexual abuse. They are forced to live their lives with an individual who destroyed their self-respect and pride, ruining their dreams and violating them in a series of horrifying moments. Whenever I hear or read about such judgements, I remember Swapna's sad, resigned face. The judgement robbed her of her self-respect and courage. She accepted it without protest or visible agitation.

The Panchayat and the villagers had never tried to put themselves in Swapna's shoes; being a girl and the only daughter of a widowed mother, her shoes perhaps seemed too small for them to wear.

Swapna therefore, was married to the man, the person responsible for her downfall. By the time they were married, six weeks after her ordeal, she was already carrying his child in her womb. Their conjugal life was uneventful since she allowed him to do whatever he wanted without a whimper. He had already turned her into a breathing plastic doll. She never spoke unless spoken to, that too in monosyllables.

She became like a zombie and never responded with any emotion to provocations or even to words of love. She had lost her ability to express her feelings. At times, she even came out of the bath inadequately clad as she would forget to put on her clothes. Like an automaton, she cooked food on time, washed and gave him clean clothes to wear; she readily tidied the house and provided him with all the facilities to entertain his friends. At night, she lay beside him like a block of ice.

Their daughter was born in due course. Swapna brought her up, ensuring that all the needs of a growing child were met. The only thing the poor child did not receive was pure motherly love or *seneh* in Assamese.

When I probed into her childhood, I discovered that Swapna grew up as a happy child. Her village Nadiapar is situated in a pristine location about 100-odd km from Bongaigaon, famous for its oil refinery and rail head. Neatly constructed tin and thatch roofed houses stood on the sides of the small gravel topped tree-lined roads. In the compound surrounding the houses were different fruit-bearing trees, including bananas, jackfruit, mangoes and coconuts. Cattle sheds with bullocks for farming and one or more milch cows were common in each household. Small country hens roamed in the courtyard, often stalked and chased by roosters. Poorly clad young children, quite a few with fat bellies because of intestinal worms, roamed the streets, playing, quarrelling, crying and laughing.

The villagers were mostly farmers, with one or two exceptions like Swapna's family. Her father was a peon in the office of the Food Corporation of India in Bongaigaon. He lived there alone and came home every weekend and on holidays. Her mother, a very efficient and hard-working housewife, looked after their small farmland and the half-acre compound. They were a happy and contented family. Swapna had two brothers younger to her whom she adored. She first studied in the lower primary village school located nearby and then in a high school about 3-km away. She pedalled to school every day, looking very attractive in the yellow *dakhana* (a long and broad loin cloth tied on the waist and flaring gradually down till the ankles), a red blouse and an *arnai* (a half-sari worn across the upper part of the body). This dress was their school uniform.

Tragedy struck when her father died unexpectedly due to a stroke. Her hardworking efficient mother shouldered all the household responsibilities, including bringing up the children. She earned a family pension from the government. Making both ends meet was not a challenge. Half the produce from their farm came to her, while the rest went to the tiller. It was sufficient to feed all of them. The villagers were always ready to help in matters that were beyond their mother's ability or reach.

They were from the Boro tribe of Assam, the original settlers of the Brahmaputra valley who constitute the largest ethnic group of Assam. The Boros hail from Tibeto-Burman stock who migrated to the valley from the trans-Himalayan region between Tibet and China in the second millennium BC. Later, they assimilated with other ethnic groups including the Aryans who migrated from the Ganges plains to Assam much later. The composite culture of Assam evolved as a result of these assimilations. However, the identity of the Boros as a separate ethnic group remained. They settled in the Brahmaputra valley, mainly concentrated across four districts of Assam.

The Bodos or Boros are a proud, cultured, well-knit society, who cherish values and maintain a rigid cultural bond. Their social mores are clean and transparent.

Swapna had grown up in an environment of inter-dependence and mutual trust. Hence, when her husband-to-be betrayed her trust, she could not bear the emotional hurt and betrayal. The damage has not fully been repaired till date.

Her conjugal life was one of subjugation. She was like a lamb left alone with a wolf. When her daughter was born, Swapna attended to her as all mothers do, doing everything possible to help her grow healthy, but she lacked the most inherent motherly traits that all mothers have. She could not love her own child like other mothers do.

Seven years after their marriage, her husband, who had turned into an alcoholic, died a painful death. A few years before his death, she started having horrifying dreams centred around ghosts visiting her home, tigers chasing her, flying with wings when vultures attacked her and even her husband gagging her so hard that she could not breathe. At times, she shrieked so loud that her daughter would start crying and her husband would yell. With lack of sleep and the resulting exhaustion, she became cagier and quieter.

After her husband's death, her mother brought her home, but her nightmares did not stop. She started hallucinating. Whenever she was alone, she felt a ferocious ghost with tiger-like teeth, blood dripping from its mouth, was stalking her. She refused to be left alone. The mother tried everything suggested by the village elders.

A sorcerer was summoned from a nearby village. He performed an elaborate exorcism to 'drive out' the 'evil spirit inhabiting her body'.

When this did not produce results, on the advice of a priest, the mother organised a *Bathow* puja and invoked Lord Shiva. She threw a sumptuous lunch for the village elders, soliciting their blessings to cure her daughter's afflictions. Nothing worked. Ultimately, she was sent to a home for women with psychological problems. She stayed there for some fifteen-odd years.

At the place, she was under treatment of a psychiatrist. Long-term medication finally worked gradually and she stopped hallucinating. But she became more reclusive and abhorred people disturbing her solitude.

In her absence, Swapna's mother brought up her grand-daughter with all the care and love the poor girl was denied by her own mother. She went on to become an energetic, vivacious, sprightly young woman who was married to a boy in Guwahati. We are told that her daughter lives with her husband and two kids within walking distance from our facilities. In the last two years since Swapna has come to live with us, she has never mentioned them to anyone. Neither has anyone from her family ever paid a visit or enquired about her; her unfortunate circumstances having made her an alien in her own family.

When her mother died of old age, Swapna, who was then forty-five, was sent back from the psychiatric care home. She stayed with her brother's family for a few years. Her sister-in-law, however, pestered her husband to find an alternative home for Swapna. One of her relatives who lived near Seneh, along with one of her friends, approached us for help. We found the lady absolutely honest and trustworthy and learnt in detail about Swapna's past. We told her that we were ready to meet Swapna to decide if we could make her a part of the Seneh family.

In a week's time, Swapna came, a petite and polite woman. We asked her questions and she responded in monosyllables. In the half-hour that she was with us, she never looked straight into our eyes. Her head was always downcast, her voice feeble, and her manners extremely polite. We decided to accommodate her on a trial basis and if we found that she was manageable, she would stay back permanently. She came, stayed back and has become a member of the Seneh family since then.

With anti-depressants and a cordial and friendly environment prevalent at Seneh, Swapna is a different woman today. She looks straight into our eyes; a thin but happy smile has replaced the morose and withdrawn look that she had when she first came to us. On the advice of the doctor who first treated her at Seneh, the anti-depressant medication has been withdrawn. She is now involved in all the activities of Seneh, including intricate embroidery work. She also helps in the kitchen. But even now, she keeps a low profile and does not open her mouth unless spoken to. Luckily, Swapna has such robust health that no one has heard her even sneeze in the last two years. When COVID recently made inroads into the Seneh family, striking all, Swapna was one of the five asymptomatic cases.

Author's Note: In reconstructing Swapna's past, I must confess, I have not done much research due to the limited conversation that Swapna allows. I went by what I was told by the lady who brought her to us and the few short conversations, I had with her. I also engaged Jutika, the Chief Care Taker, to sit with Swapna separately and try to gather whatever information she could from her. From these attempts, nothing much could be ascertained factually. Hence, quite often I used my imagination. Specifically, the detailed narratives of her mental trauma following the abduction are mainly based on my interpretations based on creative logic. My narratives are influenced by the book *Interpretation of Dreams* by Sigmund Freud that I read three decades ago, which left an indelible impression on my mind.

Anamika

A Woman From The Soundless World

The life stories of the twenty-odd women I have portrayed in this book are based on some definite leads and titbits of information I gathered from verifiable sources, including their own mouths. I stitched together this information and supplemented them, to a large extent, by my own imagination. But all my efforts to gather information or find leads about Anamika's past have ended up in dead or dark alleys. I have failed in my quest to have a cursory peek into her past, immediate or distant, so that I can embark on cobbling together a story.

The police brought Anamika to us four years back. They had no clue who she was.

She is around sixty-five years old. According to the cops, she was forcefully dropped off from a moving luxury car by someone in front of the police station at Goalpara town, 130 km away from Assam's capital city, Guwahati. A few eye-witnesses saw her being forced out of the car but unfortunately, no one took down the car number or vaguely remember even the faces of its other occupants. By the time she was brought to the police station by onlookers, all traces of the moving car had vanished. The police tried to get at the perpetrators with whatever leads they could gather, but they failed. The town had no CCTV coverage.

After three days of the incident, they rang us up and requested us to take care of her till the concerned people could be located. It is four years now, the police have failed to nab them or get any lead. I am not sure if they tried. They never came back.

When I first saw Anamika, she won my heart instantly. She is stately, tall, lean and has delicate features on a longish face. Her most striking feature and undoubtedly the most attractive, are her dazzling pair of eyes, the black eyeballs shining like stars on a clear sky, the kohl-smeared eyes intently looking at me with the eyelids fluttering over them.

With her light-brown smooth skin and the simple sari draped around her, she looked like a model of yore, who had maintained herself well. She appeared to be from a refined, middle-class background.

My eyes riveted on hers, I asked her name. She did not answer. The police woman who had escorted her told me she was completely hearing-impaired. Later, I came to know she was speech-impaired too. I was stunned and shell-shocked. There was no way one could communicate with her. I wrote down some questions, first in Assamese, and asked for answers. She looked bewildered. She did not look as if she belonged to any ethnic groups from Assam. Next, I wrote in Bengali, but elicited no response. Hindi and English queries received the same vacant look. I immediately understood the reason why the police were unsuccessful in tracing her origins. She was not only hearing and speech impaired, but she was illiterate too.

She joined the Seneh family from that day onward.

The chief caretaker suggested that we call her Anamika, meaning nameless in Assamese. I agreed. I knew it had no meaning for her, she was unable to hear it. It only helped others to identify her and us. Till today, I keep debating in my mind, if by naming her Anamika, we are making light of her fate. No word on earth, or for that matter, no sound has ever penetrated the walls God hath built around her. Those beautiful lips that can produce such an electrifying smile and the tongue that protrudes momentarily when she makes illegible sounds to express anguish or pleasure has never produced a sound that we normal beings are endowed naturally with! We should consider ourselves truly blessed.

In the last four years, she has developed a wonderful bond with me. Whenever I am around, she comes forward to meet me and tries to explain in sign language the state of her health, complain about the others, mainly about their rude behaviour or about the food. The food is normally made bland, much to her chagrin, as she likes it spicy. She comes to me and indicates that she wants to be sent home. But when I take a map and ask her in sign language to identify the place where she wants me to take her, she can't pinpoint anything.

Often she indicated a train journey that will lead her home. I obtained a railway map and asked her to show me where she wants to go. She looked confused. She also conveyed in her peculiar sign language that she has four children by pointing her index finger at child visitors who throng the place, and then lifting four fingers. She is especially restless when the mango season is around. She points her index finger to the mangoes hanging from the tree in Seneh's courtyard. We perceive she is trying to convey that she has plenty of mangoes at her place and she is keen to go and get mangoes for all of us from her home.

She looks very happy when I am around and constantly tries to demand my full attention. At times, it becomes a challenge for our support staff to keep her away from me, especially when I am busy with office work. I spend an average of three to four hours at Seneh every day.

Once, when I was writing something, she indicated that she can write too. I was elated. Maybe we will be able to trace her origins. I gave her the pen and asked her to write something. She wrote a few alphabets. I immediately identified it as a south Indian script. I took the help of a few friends from the four south Indian states. A Telugu-speaking friend identified the letters as Telugu script. I almost jumped in jubilation. At last, we were in a position to trace her origins and probably reunite her with her family.

But alas! When a Telugu-speaking gentleman wrote a few questions like asking her to write her name, or her son's name or her place of origin, she gave a blank look and looked at him in bewilderment. She wrote something, but it conveyed nothing. He tried repeatedly but what she wrote was some more alphabets that did not form or convey any word. We were thoroughly disappointed. We tried a number of times but all in vain.

We pasted her photograph on Facebook, put it up on our webpage and wrote both to the Director General of Police of Telangana and Andhra Pradesh but we drew a blank. We have failed to locate her origins. She keeps pestering us to send her home, but we are helpless without any leads.

We have discovered something. She is immensely talented in her own way. She can dance, rock her head like a Bharat Natyam dancer and mimic everyone, as well as protest at any form of injustice. She wears her dress elegantly, sits through the daily prayers in rapt attention and cooks perfect *idlis*. She can also cook another popular south Indian dish, *rasam*.

She mimics how I keep drawing my trousers up as they slide down because of my bulging waistline. It results in peels of laughter from all around. Honestly, that has forced me to buy suspenders now to keep my pants anchored in the right place.

Anamika has gradually reconciled to her fate. She has started enjoying the company of the other residents of the home and has developed a special bonding with Jutika, our Chief Caretaker. When we organised a cultural function to celebrate our raising day, Anamika took part in two group dances along with the others. She even modelled in a well-choreographed fashion parade.

Although she never heard the accompanying music, it was amazing how she managed to keep the rhythm with others, and also, on the catwalk. Draped in a colourful sari, which she wore like a rural woman in interior Telangana, with an earthen pitcher on her head, delicately supported by her arm, she elicited loud applause from the 300-odd spectators. They appreciated her perfection and grace. The spectators did not know about her disabilities.

Unfortunately, at the time of writing this piece, Anamika is not keeping well. First, she started losing weight suddenly within a span of a few months. She has lost her appetite too. The main problems in diagnosing her ailment by the doctors is her inability to communicate about her symptoms. After a series of blood tests, ultrasound and CAT scan, the doctors have found that her liver is enlarged alarmingly. We have consulted doctors of three different hospitals. With medication, her appetite has since improved but her ankles swell often without any manifesting pains. Off and on, with medication, the swellings reduce, but reappear repeatedly. She is now almost reduced to skin and bones. It pains me when she limps up to me and shows me her swollen feet. I try to assure her that it will be alright soon, although I am not convinced myself, either. I am sure my readers will join me in praying for her recovery. According to the hepatologist, the prognosis is not encouraging. I can only hope and pray he is proved wrong and that by the time you read this, she comes out victorious.

And lo and behold, by the time I am ready with my manuscript, her appetite is resurfacing. She is also gaining some weight. She is her radiant vibrant self again.

Lazwanti

Even Dementia Can't Put Her Down

The checkered keelback, locally known as *dhora* in Assam, is a water snake known for its scary hissing. It's a non-poisonous reptile, and its only self-protective mechanism other than taking recourse to fleeing fast and swimming zigzag, is to hiss menacingly when cornered; the hiss is so loud and full-throated, that the weak-hearted will surely panic. I can bet that unless you recognise the snake to be the harmless keelback, you will take to your heels. Unless you are the aggressive, brave type, who attacks a potential enemy before it strikes, you will be quick to grab a long stick to bludgeon it to death.

I am sure, the reader is confused wondering how suddenly from a story writer, I have turned into an ophiologist. What relevance do descriptions of snakes have to do with the profiles of women living at Seneh? Have patience and you will soon understand why suddenly I am remembering the *dhora* snake before portraying Lazwanti's life story. At the outset, let me express my displeasure to the one who named her Lazwanti. This lady who was born into a peasant family in a nondescript village in Bihar, is anything but a *lajwanti*—meaning one who is shy and timid.

At seventy plus, Lazwanti is a miniature of a woman—not more than four feet and a couple of inches tall. Not only is she short, she is thin and extremely sprightly for her age. The ease with which Janmoni, the four feet ten inches tall, young, ebullient, thin, in-house nurse lifts her up, as if she is a rubber doll, gives the impression that her weight may not be more than 25-30 kg. Even while asleep, the omnipresent veil that she wraps so meticulously around her head has never dared to slip away, fearing strong intervention from her frail, shaking hands. The veil also hides half of her forehead at all times and this prevents me from writing more about her looks. A woman's hairdo is the first item that strikes one when you look at her. But in Lazwanti's case, I saw her hair and her ears only once.

It has been three years since she joined the Seneh family. The face that looks out of the veil is enigmatic. Even at this age, her facial skin is taut and unblemished except for the area over her lips that earlier covered her teeth. With all the teeth gone, this portion of her facial skin is loose and wrinkled. You can't miss her long prominent nose and her brilliant eyes, greyish black in colour, that flit around like that of a rabbit. The most significant trait of her persona, however, is her abrasive vocabulary. She can utter no sentence without the Assamese version of a four-letter word embedded within it. When provoked, her vulgar words breach all boundaries. Unfortunately, she gets provoked on the flimsiest of grounds.

Let me quote some examples. Her only hobby, yes, you have read correctly, her hobby is swabbing. She will swab and then re-swab the same area a number of times. She will not stop even if she is ordered: 'Stop that'. When she is asked to stop swabbing by someone, she erupts with the most abrasive language and belittles the person in such a way that he or she loses the courage to meet anyone's eyes. Her words will not spare even the secret parts of your mother or sister.

The other reasons that will ruffle all her feathers is if you ask her to bathe and wear a clean sari. She will erupt like a volcano and spit out molten lava on you. It is an amusing sight to see the young nurse, Janmoni, lifting her and carrying her to the bath. Lazwanti will be livid, pounding Janmoni's back like a drum with her clenched fists and swearing; you think, she will certainly kill her the moment Janmoni puts her down on the bathroom

also heard about a monthly market in Maithili-speaking Muzaffarpur district of Bihar, where prospective grooms were prominently seated on a platform with their qualifications and abilities and their family backgrounds written on a placard for the girl's side to come and bid. And of course, the highest bidder got the man.

I cannot vouch for its authenticity, since I never saw it myself. I come from a region where, from time immemorial, dowry is not practised. Hence, I have learnt to consider it the ugliest practice and the biggest blot on Indian society.

It was a common practice in those days to have nautch girls put up a dance show for the groom's party in Bihar. I have personally attended weddings with such a show.

Lazwanti was married off to this boy of sixteen when she was nine. However, she was not allowed to go to her in-laws' place, even once, nor was her husband allowed to visit her, until she attained puberty.

***

In my childhood in a village in the early fifties, there lived a gentleman about 200 yards from our house, a small-time tea farmer who owned an old Morris Minor car. His was the only car in the area at that time. So it was a marvel for us and we would run to the gravelled main road whenever we heard the sound of its engine approaching or saw the mushrooming cloud of dust it threw up on the road as it went past. In the mornings, starting the engine was a challenge. At times, the ignition key worked and the car came to life immediately without hesitation. If it did not, the next alternative was to crank the engine with a shoulder-breaking handle. And if that did not work either, it had to be pushed manually for the engine to cough out trails of black smoke from its exhaust as it spluttered to life. As a boy, I looked forward to such opportunities to join the pushing brigade. It was an exhilarating thrill when the car eventually revved up and drove off.

When I decided to pen Lazwanti's life, and sat with her to learn about her past life, she behaved exactly like the Morris Minor. For example, the engine started instantly when I asked about her married life and more specifically, about her husband. She was ready with lucid memories as soon as the ignition key was turned. Her garrulous and gauche efforts to disgrace her husband in the most venomous and vile manner would start immediately. Her outbursts would overflow all boundaries. Often, she compared him to an ox for whom relationships did not matter so long as there was a cow to mount. However, most of the adjectives she used to describe him are unprintable.

Within a few months of their conjugal life together,

she conceived and delivered a baby girl. Unfortunately, when the baby was three months old, the infant died during a smallpox epidemic. Thereafter, she could not bear any children. She was declared barren and discarded like one brushes off a fly that is found hovering over a prematurely ripe mango. I once again refrain from using the vulgar words she used for her husband. However, his act of using and abandoning her in the wilderness must have left an indelible scar on her psyche. Whenever I tried to obtain more information about her past, her shrill rants against her husband would begin. Only when done, did she pay attention to what I wanted to know.

Coming back to my Morris Minor analogy, when I asked Lazwanti questions about her past, she refrained from giving any answer initially. She would give a distant, bewildered, vacant look and get lost in her own thoughts. If I kept pressing, like attempting to start the engine with the handle, she would suddenly come to life and start talking disjointedly about her past. It was a difficult task to piece her story together and come to a definite chronological order. Whenever I asked her husband's whereabouts, she had no definite answer. I presumed her husband was dead because one day she told Janmoni how she had peed on the place where the last rites of her husband were performed. Another proof, she does not wear any vermillion on her forehead.

Whenever I failed to cajole her to reply to my probing

questions, I took the help of the chief caretaker and the young nurse. They would push her to talk with threats of an immediate bath or on the pretext of taking away her old clothes that she had preserved in an old metal box she had brought along. From experience, they knew these threats unnerved her. Here the analogy of pushing the Morris Minor fits in. At such times, she would be terribly angry, curse her husband and in-laws in the crudest vulgar words and then relent. She would then answer the questions, although there was hardly any coherence or continuity in what she blurted out.

We held umpteen probing sessions with her over six months. Whatever information we could gather about her past in these sessions, were in snatches. I have joined the dots in the best way possible. I admit, it is a patchwork of a novice. Nevertheless, I am inclined to believe, her life followed the following road.

The peasant family she was born into was neither poor nor wealthy. Her father and his three brothers together tilled the cultivable land they owned that yielded multiple crops like paddy, wheat, malt, maize and pulses. The yield was sufficient to feed their nineteen-member family. It also generated sufficient money through sales of the surplus yield to cater for other expenditures. The family had more boys than girls, which they considered an economic booster for the future of the family. They had four milch cows and two pairs of bullocks to pull the plough, pump out the ground water from the shallow well for irrigation and drive the bullock cart that was used for both transporting the farm produce and also to ferry the kids and the women folk whenever needed. She had a happy childhood.

All this changed when she got married at the tender age of nine. Until thirteen, she was at home, and not allowed to roam around freely unless accompanied by an older woman of the family. She was constantly reminded that she was someone else's property kept with them for safe custody. Open defecation in the fields was the norm but for her, there was the rider that however urgent the need be, she was not to go alone and wait for an older woman to accompany her. A sari, that remained a challenge for her to manage, overnight replaced her frock. She was forced to learn housekeeping, including cooking and washing clothes. It was goodbye to running around, games, and other childhood pranks. Her tender mind revolted. She became a parrot in a cage.

Three years after her marriage, her grandfather died. All the male members of the family including toddlers and even babes-in-arms were required to shave off their heads except for a small tuft at the rear, that looked like a miniature ponytail. Pulling the ponytails of the boys of their household, unnoticed by her elders, was her only clandestine entertainment in those otherwise gloomy days.

Although her menstrual periods started six months thereafter, luckily for her, the demise of her grandfather delayed her departure to her marital home. As per custom, the bride can go to her in-laws only after a year after the demise of any member of the bride's family.

Her in-laws were good people. Her husband's elder sister was already married off. His two elder brothers with their families and a younger sister four years her junior lived under the same roof. She described her husband as vile, a demon, an incarnation of Ravana, with an excessive animal urge to torment her sexually.

A couple of years after her arrival, her husband departed for Guwahati to live and look after the fields of his childless maternal uncle.

Her memory here on is blurred. We tried repeatedly to know where her maternal uncle-in-law stayed at Guwahati. In the fifties, Guwahati was a small town with a population of less than 25,000 surrounded by cultivable land, forests and numerous water bodies covered with green hyacinth. Today, they have all been mercilessly encroached upon without any planning to preserve the ecosystem. Guwahati now has thirty lakh inhabitants. Consequently, the former town once surrounded by green hills, has turned into a concrete jungle.

When her husband left for Guwahati, she was six months pregnant. She delivered a baby girl after a full term. There was more gloom than rejoicing in the family.

A girl was considered a huge liability and drain on the family's fortunes.

She said that her 'bull of a husband' who was too busy with other hens at Guwahati, never even saw the face of their child, who died when she was just three months old in a smallpox epidemic with some other children and grownups of the village.

Lazwanti has scattered memories about the epidemic. 'The disease claimed many lives from the village, mainly children. A few lost their eyesight,' she recalled. Then suddenly she clamped up as if struck by lightning. Our proddings fell on deaf ears. Instead, she shook her head to convey her annoyance and withdrew into her shell like a tortoise.

The gap between her then and now was difficult to bridge. She said she joined her husband at Guwahati and they were together for some time. Her maternal uncle-in-law was a nice person; he and his wife had no children and had enough land to plough. She helped them in the farming and cooked for all. But when her husband's name cropped up, she began lashing out at him again. 'The bastard threw me out and had the temerity to call me barren. The son-of-a-bitch's grandpa never taught him how to sire a child,' she began in a brazen, vulgar tirade against her husband. We had to forcibly stop her outbursts.

The next session was peaceful. We decided to make

her talk coherently, without mentioning her husband's name and ensuring that her thoughts did not wander towards him.

Lazwanti often wets her bed, then invariably says she did it because she was pissing on her dead husband's body. Actually, she has no control over her bladder. The nurses forcibly make her wear an adult diaper. She hates it and often throws it off quietly. Often, at night, she relieves herself on the floor by the side of her bed. Against vehement protests, she is forced to mop up the stinking puddles. She never admits that it is her doing.

In spite of over a dozen sessions thereafter, we failed to elicit any more coherent information. What we did gather is that she left her maternal in-law's home (we could not ascertain whether she was driven out or if she left voluntarily) and started living in a *jhuggi* (slum) cluster, working as a part-time maid and also begging to eke out a living. Later, she started working full-time in a house as a live-in maid. The lady of the house was very compassionate and cordial. She stayed there for a long time.

Then her employer secured employment for her in a women's clubhouse, where her job was to clean the place and serve tea to the members when they met to play cards every evening. Her other duties included guarding the house and the compound, mainly from stray cattle. She got accommodation in the clubhouse itself and had a small kitchen for cooking. Members of the club, chiefly its president, were very fond of her and cared for her welfare. The president actually owned the property and allowed the members to use it as a meeting place.

With advancing age and with the onset of dementia, leaving Lazwanti alone in the clubhouse, especially at night, became untenable. Hence, they decided to find a place where Lazwanti could safely live for the rest of her life. The president and a few members came and met us. Initially, we were reluctant. We were getting plenty of requests to accommodate full-time maids who had become more a liability than an asset to the household because of advancing age and ill health. As a rule, we despised such requests. We were even more suspicious because the ladies who pleaded with us to accommodate Lazwanti even promised to compensate us.

Before making a commitment, we sent out a fact-finding team. The team's report was encouraging.

Lazwanti became a resident of Seneh soon after. We never accepted the offer of the club for financial compensation. Till two years thereafter, the president of the club often dropped in to inquire about Lazwanti. Unfortunately, Lazwanti often does not recognise her.

Author's Note: Months after I wrote this piece, one winter morning, I found Lazwanti basking in the sun on a stool all alone and gazing vacantly and unblinkingly at nothing in particular. It was the gaze of a distant soul, forlorn and aimless. It appeared to me that she was not aware of her surroundings. Her lips were open, reminding me of a fish. For the first time in my association with her, the veil had slipped off unobstructed, exposing her head and her left arm completely. What struck me first was the skin of her arm above her elbow. It was like loose-hanging wrinkly dough.

This skin must once have held taut some real muscles. It proved that in her prime, she was not the skin and bone that I had imagined her to be. The next was her hair. It was a wild thick fog of grey, a short and unruly tuft. That, in no way, explained the few hanging strands I noticed earlier. On inquiry, I was told that when all efforts to eradicate the lice in her hair failed, her long hair was shorn off like an unruly grassy lawn, not long ago, by our nurses, albeit forcefully.

No wonder, routinely, she curses our nurses in her signature obnoxious tongue. She mostly singles out poor Janmoni. She also does it because, on another level, there is a beautiful bonding between the two. Janmoni is the only one whom she trusts with the key to the old steel box I mentioned earlier. It has never been opened even once since she arrived.

Only she knows what is inside the box. She is decidedly possessive about it! One theory doing the rounds by the other residents, who are all as inquisitive as the mouse in the Tom and Jerry cartoon series, is that there will be some ornaments in it. It is extremely unlikely, because she often curses some of her old acquaintances, whose names she cannot recall of having made off with her jewellery.

What a darling of a woman she is!

Kusum Deka

Tossed Around By The Tide, But Still Smiling

She was only a little over twelve years old. A mischievous child, she ran about with her friends, climbed trees, stole mangoes, jumped into the river from its embankment like a riverine frog, and was always able to remain longer underwater by holding her breath than the others. There were six of them of the same age group. They played *Kutkut Kabaddi* or the *Rumal Lukua* (two games played by girls in rural Assam). I have explained in the chapter on Tulumai how *Kut Kabbadi* is played. In *Rumaal Lukua,* the participants sit on their haunches in a circle, both hands on the ground in front; the leader takes a *rumaal* (handkerchief) and runs around behind the seated girls. She drops the handkerchief behind one of them stealthily, while still running. If, before she finishes the circle, the girl behind whom the *rumaal* is dropped, does not find it by instinct, she gets a good smack on her back. The player thereafter collects the *rumaal* and starts running, her place taken by the previous runner.

One day, while playing *Rumaal Lukua*, the diminutive, exuberant, energetic, ever-smiling Kusum, suddenly experienced some liquid trickling down her thighs. The others noticed it too. When told about it, she started howling. Someone ran to her mother to inform her. The experienced mother understood what had happened. Taking a long cloth, she ran to the spot, wrapped Kusum in it, and brought her home. On the way, she explained to her daughter that what had happened was a natural phenomenon for girls of her age. It was as natural as the sun rising every morning or the trees shedding their old leaves every spring making way for new leaves. She had come of age. The mother said she had not expected it to happen so early, so she had put off her plans to forewarn Kusum.

At home, a small room was immediately vacated and a straw bed made on the floor. Kusum was asked to live there alone and as per the custom, she was not to set her eyes on anyone from the opposite sex until all the ceremonies were over. Even her father and her kid brother were forbidden from entering the room or looking at her.

The village astrologer was consulted. Based on the position of the planets at the time when the first flow started, he calculated the period of her quarantine, which varied from four to seven days. The astrologer decreed that it would be five days of quarantine. During this period, the rules did not permit her any cereals or cooked food. She was to live on fruits and milk only. She was not allowed to venture out of the room except for calls of nature and a bath. When out, looking on any male was blasphemy.

On the second day, a delicate box made of thin bamboo strips, finely seasoned and polished, was brought. This box is called *jopa* in the local language and is available in the rural markets. In a new *gamosa* (a woven thin white towel, with red flowers adorning its four sides, the flowers woven with coloured yarn) some paddy, a *tamol* and a *paan* (areca nut and betel leaf) and a pen knife were artfully tied into a neat bundle. The bundle was placed inside the *jopa* and the lid closed. Then, it was sent to the house of her closest female friend to be kept there in a secluded clean place for the quarantine period. No one was allowed to open it.

On the morning of the fifth day, six to seven married women in traditional attire arrived from the neighbourhood (widows are debarred from taking part in the festivities). Her mother made a paste of raw turmeric, soaked black gram and a little mustard oil. Her father made a special bath, square-shaped, with four tender banana trees, cut above their roots, as the corner pillars. The platform was made of finely woven strips of banana tree barks.

A garland of mango leaves was tied around the bath. The ladies surrounded the bath with a *chadar* (half sari) and then sang *Biya Naam* (folk songs sung in marriage ceremonies) accompanied by repeated *urulis*, a sound made by the women together by rolling their tongues. The vibrating sound is considered auspicious for all religious functions of Assam and Bengal. Kusum was undressed and the paste smeared on her tender body. She then got the ceremonial bath.

Before the bath, her mother went to the river to collect water in a pitcher accompanied by other women in a procession. The ladies sang in perfect tune, praising the Lord, all along the route. First, the collected water was poured on her head followed by regular water to complete the bath. Her body was then dried with a new *gamosa*. Thereafter, she was dressed in colourful silk apparel and adorned like a bride. Shortly afterward, the *jopa* arrived on the head of a young *kumari*, a virgin girl, accompanied by the elder ladies of the young girl's household and a few friends.

The entourage was received at the gate that had two banana trees standing on the two ends of the gate, with a garland of mango leaves tied across, joining both. A low wooden broad platform, called a *pira,* was placed in the middle, and the *jopa* placed reverently on it. The women who gave the bath came in a procession, with the mother leading them to receive the *jopa,* like she would have received the bridegroom in a traditional Assamese marriage. All of them together with the women singing hymns then brought the *jopa* home ceremoniously. Thereafter, everyone present was treated with a sumptuous meal.

This ceremony over, a feast was laid for the invitees lasting the whole day. The invitees came with gifts for the girl. Without actually understanding the rationale of the ceremony, Kusum was excited about the presents. In return, she offered each invitee a *tamul paan* (sliced areca nut and betel leaf) from a brass plate with a finely chiselled stem called *bota*. Kusum enjoyed the attention.

The ceremony changed Kusum forever. After the special restrictions of the first five days were over, her life was scripted differently. There was now a dos and don'ts lists, clipping her wings permanently. Unfortunately, the 'do not' list was so long that it took all her will power and determination to follow it. Frocks were banned and she was allowed only a *chador* and *mekhela*. Climbing trees was not only forbidden but impossible with the new dress code. Leapfrogging into the river bed for a swim was not in the 'can do' list, either. Meeting older boys or going out alone at night was not permitted. She was told that playing childhood games was taboo as 'You are no longer a girl:

you are a woman.' Overnight, Kusum had graduated from a girl to a woman in the eyes of all her elders.

In the dos list came cooking, cleaning, sweeping, swabbing, washing clothes, pounding rice to make *pitha* (rice cake) and other household work; knitting and weaving were other musts. In a short span of time, she became adept at performing her assigned duties, although she was not much of a cook. Fortunately, her father came to her rescue. He was so dissatisfied with her performance that he ordered her mother not to let her cook unless unavoidable.

Her father's name was Govinda Deka. He was a tiny man, not more than five feet and a quarter; he was dark, thin and perky, with an oval-shaped face, two small sunken eyes and protruding cheekbones. Every morning at six, he rode his old bicycle, carrying two jute bags hanging from the handles on each side. The right-hand bag was full with tea leaves, sugar, some biscuits, a few packets of buns from the previous day's leftovers and two freshly washed *gamosas* of thick cotton yarn. The other bag contained a two-litre can of kerosene and some old soiled cleaning clothes.

He cycled every day to the nearest bus stand 6-km away to sell tea. He had a small three-side open kiosk with an old rusted cast iron roof and bamboo posts erected on the side of the road, where he laid a table with two benches placed on both sides. Here, he made and sold tea. The bus stand was opposite a government office with about twenty-odd employees. The police outpost was also close by.

He kept his other merchandise like a kerosene stove, a saucepan black with soot, an aluminium kettle, a strainer, a metal mug and ten small glasses and also the table and benches in the custody of the office watchman at night. For this favour, the watchman got four cups of tea and a bun free of cost every day. After setting up the shop, her father made tea, and sold it to people waiting for the bus or those visiting the office. He also carried tea for the staff in the office as well as the police outpost and sold it there. A vendor on a bicycle laden with packed buns supplied him the buns, which he further sold at a profit along with the tea.

The earnings from his tea shop were sufficient to support his wife and three children: Kusum and her two younger brothers. In fact, his wife had given birth to one more daughter who died when she was just seven days old, because of yellow fever. Making both ends meet had never been a big challenge for Govinda Deka, except during the rains.

Like all others of his village, he dreaded this season. Within fifteen days of the start of the monsoon, the river Goreng flowing by the side of their village swelled with the fury of a hungry tigress in captivity that had suddenly broken loose, foaming and roaring. Everything in its path was swallowed up by the angry river. It lashed against its banks with such fury that the alluvial soil on the sides could not withstand its fury. Huge chunks broke loose. To protect the villages, the government constructed some embankments with hard soil and sand-filled bags. But could nature's fury be resisted with such trivial measures?

When the river was in spate, the villagers mounted a vigil round the clock, with sand bags to stop the current breaching the embankment at vulnerable places. But when they found this was not possible, they would rush to alert the villagers in the low-lying areas to evacuate and move to higher grounds. Unfortunately, Kusum's house was not only in a low-lying area, it was also near the river.

As a rule, the family was prepared for such an eventuality. When they saw the river in spate, they packed their knick-knacks, clothes, utensils, a lantern with enough kerosene in a can, foodstuff for two weeks, a tarpaulin piece, a few bamboo poles and some fodder for the cows. They were ready to move to a safer place as soon as the signal from the watchful volunteers was relayed by word of mouth. At times, her father took this decision himself, after taking stock of the river's fury and the expected deluge. The villagers trusted his foresight. The family also had a raft made of banana trunk handy, to navigate to higher places, if required. It was a routine affair for the villagers yet a matter of life and death, that occurred almost every third year. The experienced elders could predict the probability of an unabated deluge on the onset of the monsoon itself.

The evacuation involved moving out to the side of the nearest highway. Her father and brothers pitched a tent with the bamboo poles and the tarpaulin. The makeshift tent provided enough space for five of them to squeeze in and to keep the stove and the utensils for cooking and eating in a corner. Bedsheets, torn blankets and jute bags compensated for walls. This nomadic phase varied from year to year. At times, it was short, but sometimes it lasted for a month or so. Relief provided by the state was always late in arriving and also insufficient. If they survived, it was because of their far-sightedness and grit.

For the children, it was carnival time. They played on the road the whole day, at times drenched to the skin by the rains, till the parents shouted at them to take cover. The children would descend on the approaching relief truck and then crowd around the rear of the vehicle when it stopped, like a swarm of locusts. They would receive the relief materials on behalf of their parents. Quite often, the children were chased away by the suppliers, who invariably shouted at the crowd to maintain discipline.

Until she attained puberty, the agile young Kusum could slide through the crowding children to reach the truck first. After she matured, she was not only forbidden to jostle in a crowd, or play in the rain, but was also handicapped by ankle-length *mekhela*, an impediment to running faster without tumbling face down.

Kusum grew up to full womanhood a short and slender woman, with hair so long, if left loose and combed back, it touched her knees.

Even today at around seventy, her hair is still black with only a few streaks of grey. She has a small oval head with a pair of glittering eyes, perfectly curved fluffy eyebrows, a prominent sharp nose, small bow-shaped lips always with a permanent pout, that hide a pair of regular, finely crafted small white teeth. Her light whitish brown taut skin has only one blemish a tiny protrusion over her left cheekbone. She looks pleasant, almost perky. She also has a peculiar gait, as if her left leg is unable to keep up with the energy of the right, probably because it is shorter than the right.

'I cannot forget that fateful bright and sunny autumn day,' narrated Kusum. 'I was around fifteen and my mother decided to take me along with her to the Lord Krishna temple a few miles away. We took a bus after walking two miles to the bus stop,' she said, with moist eyes, the eyeballs downcast. 'It was a Sunday and my father was home. When we returned home, we found a large gathering in our courtyard. My father was lying sprawled on the small bed, the bedding soaked with fresh blood. There was blood everywhere, on the floor and on the bed.' Her father most probably had an ulcer in his stomach that had burst. The villagers rushed him to the nearest hospital on a bullock cart, with her mother and eldest son trotting behind. But before they could reach the Primary Health Centre, he breathed his last.

An uncle travelled 200 km to oversee the ritualistic arrangements. Thereafter, he helped his eldest nephew restart his father's tea stall business and left.

Initially out of pity and because of the reputation of his father as a quality tea brewer, sales soared. But the lad had no experience and the quality of the tea that he brewed was mediocre. So after the initial euphoria, sales dwindled and finally he had to shut shop. He migrated with another friend to Guwahati, and as time passed, he severed his umbilical cord. Left to fend for themselves, the mother started working as a part-time housemaid. She took Kusum along to assist her, save on the days when she had her periods.

The younger brother worked in the planting season as a ploughman, guiding the bullocks to pull the plough back and forth in the fields. The job was seasonal. For the remaining months, he had to find work elsewhere. That ultimately forced him to leave the village for better opportunities, leaving the mother-daughter alone to fend for themselves.

When she was sixteen, Kusum's mother decided it was time for Kusum to get married. She enlisted the help of her brother-in-law. On his advice, they left for his place of residence, where Kusum was paraded before a jaunty-looking young man attired in dhoti-kurta and lavishly sprayed with cheap perfume, the smell mildly stirring her sensory nerves. He came with his father, a balding portly man, his teeth brownish-red because of his habit of chewing betel leaf smeared with edible lime and raw tobacco. Elaborate arrangements were made to welcome them. Special snacks called *pitha* were made of a paste of the sticky *bora* rice powder and molasses, and fried in mustard oil. In addition, a sweet was made by baking the rice powder over the hearth and then rolling it with sweetened coconut or sesame seed powder as stuffing inside. There were also round sweets of desiccated coconut called *narikol laru* and a broth of sweet-smelling *joha* rice with milk, sugar and dry fruits served cold called *payax*.

The main dish *sira doi* comprised of beaten rice made from *Malbhog* paddy and curd sweetened with molasses.

Although Kusum hardly had any hand in preparing the fare, her aunt boasted to the visitors that almost everything served was Kusum's handiwork. This innocuous lie later proved to be a nightmare for Kusum.

After the sumptuous meal, the father-son duo sat back. It was time to usher in the bride-to-be. In came Kusum, led by her aunt, in a silk dress, teamed up with a red blouse, her hair neatly done, eyes blackened with *kohol*, a *bindi* on her forehead and face powdered with talcum. She was coached to walk slowly and soundlessly. She wore a pair of gold bangles on her hands and an additional pair of glass bangles on her right hand. She came in holding a brass *bota* with sliced areca nut and beetle leaf, jellied lime and *dhapat* (raw, dried chunks of tobacco leaf).

She was so nervous that her right hand shook uncontrollably, making a clanging noise from the bangles.

He was mild, his manners timid, his voice low. He ran a provision shop in a small town, with zest and alacrity. Like Kusum, he was nervous. She bowed to the father, touching his feet; she offered him a *gamosa* and the *bota* with its contents to pick from, and then walked towards the young man and offered him the *bota*. He looked intently at her face, his eyes never betraying what he was thinking. His father prompted him to ask her a few questions of his own choosing. He was shaken by this sudden turn of events. He was dumbstruck. Bewildered and lost, gasping in nervousness, the only question he asked her was her name, which he already knew.

The interview and presentations over, the father-son duo left. The astrologer would decide the date for the wedding. He would calculate an auspicious day based on their zodiac signs and position of the planets at the time of their birth.

They were married three months later in a ceremony akin to the one she went through at the onset of puberty, except that in lieu of the *jopa*, this time it was the groom in flesh and blood, elegantly attired in a silk kurta and a fine cotton dhoti. He shaved neatly. His hairdo included a lavish use of scented hair oil. He wore a garland of *tulsi* leaves on his head. They took the marital vows in front of the sacred fire, the *howan*, amid chanting of Sanskrit hymns by the priest. Celebrations followed and the groom's party was treated like royalty.

She joined her husband's family. A total of twelve people lived under the same roof. Her in-laws, her eldest brother-in-law, a vegetable vendor, with his wife and two kids, a second brother who worked as a farmhand and his wife and son, and, finally their younger sister. They lived in harmony and everyone respected and obeyed the parents. 'My mother-in-law was most considerate and loving, with a heart of gold. She was just the kind of person every daughter-in-law living in a joint family should have,' said Kusum. 'My husband had his small business at Golaghat, about 250 km away. He came home every month for two days.'

Then, Kusum with a wry smile narrated to me her discomfiture when her mother-in-law asked her to cook the rice. After all, the family was made to believe that Kusum was an accomplished cook. 'I knew how to wash the rice and put in the right amount of water. But I did not know for how long it is to be boiled or how to drain off the water. So when the rice started boiling, I started howling uncontrollably. My mother-in-law came in immediately to ask what was wrong. I sobbingly explained my dilemma. She mumbled something about what the aunt had said...then she stopped mid-sentence with a knowing smile. She patiently showed me the process. From that day onward, I became her apprentice.'

Kusum wished she could see her husband more often. She missed him. Another cause of dismay were the taunts and mockery thrown at her by her eldest, irritatingly vocal sister-in-law. She did it always when the mother-in-law was absent. Perhaps this was jealousy because Kusum was the darling of their mother-in-law. Other than these two reasons, her life in the family was eventless and peaceful until both her in-laws died within a span of six months. In the interim, she had had a daughter, who was six then. The girl kept her busy and filled the void created by her husband's absence. Her eldest brother-in-law now became the head of the family. He was a just and considerate man, but the same could not be said of his wife.

When the brother-in-law came home after the day's work, exhausted and tired, he wanted peace and tranquillity. But his sharp-tongued wife was full of vitriolic diatribes against Kusum. Out of exasperation, and against his better judgement, he made Kusum the target of his harshness. Exactly for the same reason, her second brother-in-law also deserted the family with his wife and children and started living elsewhere.

'I never complained to my husband about what had

been happening in the family when he came home. I wanted him to be happy and content so that we could spend the few days he stayed in harmony,' said Kusum. 'When his sister-in-law complained about me to my husband, he brushed it aside with a silent nod and before departing, always advised me not to cross swords with her and to bear her silently.'

Unfortunately, it was just the beginning of her tale of woe. Her husband suffered a massive stroke at Golaghat and died a sudden death. At that juncture, their daughter was ten years old. When his lifeless body was brought to their home in the back of a dilapidated mini truck, she looked at it and fainted. When she regained consciousness, she was numb at first, till the tears from her sunken eyes started flowing down in torrents. She wailed, beating her chest.

Let me narrate the absurd and ignominious social edicts a rural woman in western Assam has to endure if her husband dies before her. For the first four days, from the date of the demise, she is allowed a single dress to wear—a white, cotton *mekhela* and *chador*. She is forced to wear this for four days and nights. She is also forced to take a bath in it. She has to keep wearing the wet garment till it dries out of its own on her grief-stricken body.

If the weather is humid, it remains wet almost throughout. The widow is even denied a *gamosa*. She is forced to sleep with the wet dress on a bed of hay on the ground, and when awake, keep sitting on it, with nothing to eat or drink except water. She cannot comb her hair. After attending nature's call, she has to bathe again. In winter, a simmering fire by her bedside is what keeps her warm at night. No blanket. From the fifth day onwards, Kusum was allowed a change of clothes and a bland meal a day without oil, onion or garlic. This continued until the thirteenth day when with a sumptuous feast, the mourning period came to an end. From then on, their custom dictated only white dress for the widow, no non-vegetarian food for the rest of her life. (All Assamese eat non-veg food irrespective of caste or religion.)

Social taboos for widowed women in our country can be repressive, especially in rural households. Kusum by then was thirty-five, and she had to quietly accept all these draconian social rules. To add to her grief, her sister-in-law started making her life miserable. Quite often, even her daughter was denied food. She decided that enough was enough.

Her brother-in-law lacked the courage to take a stand against his wife. Even the schooling of her daughter stopped because she had no means to pay her fees. She was forced to work like a slave, and even her young daughter could not escape the tyranny and wrath of her sister-in-law. She started looking for an escape route.

Her brother who lived in Guwahati heard about her plight and came to her rescue. He took both of them to

Guwahati to live with him and admitted her daughter to a nearby school. Kusum found a job as a part-time maid. Life was eventless and peaceful until her daughter, who dropped out of school at fifteen, expressed her resolve to marry a twenty-five-year-old chauffer.

The couple was married, and started living in a rented accommodation away from their house. Her grandson was born two years later. The daughter asked her mother to live with her to take care of her newborn child. When the child was a year old, Kusum returned to her brother.

'With three children and my brother's income stagnating, life was tough. I could not get a job as a part-time house cleaner in the locality to help him. Also, my daughter kept pestering me to live with her. So, I left my brother's house, much against his will, to live with my daughter.'

Her son-in-law picked up a job away from home and started living alone there, coming home every month for a day or two. He would give his wife money to meet the expenditure for the month and go back. One day, he came home drunk. All of a sudden, Kusum found her soft-spoken, amiable and sober son-in-law a changed man: abusive, abrasive and aggressive.

Things went downhill from this point. Whenever the son-in-law came home, there was discord and disharmony. The family was in disarray, they suffered untold hardships. Her daughter became abusive and impatient and the grandson disobedient.

To help her daughter, Kusum started working as a part-time housemaid in two houses. It was back-breaking work that included sweeping, swabbing, washing utensils and clothes for Rs 2,000 per month from each house. The daughter too wanted to work, but the husband would have none of it. He threatened to stop coming or giving her even the paltry sum he left behind when he came, if she did.

Eventually, Kusum developed a nagging backache and this made it impossible for her to sweep and swab the floors or wash clothes. She lost both her jobs.

She was rendered helpless. She was unable to decide what to do, where to go.

'Then I decided I must work to earn whatever little I can to help my daughter and grandson. With a bad back and advancing old age, the only line of work was begging. I selected a place near the entrance to the local temple, spread a jute bag to sit on and started begging. It was not a bad decision. On an average, I earned twenty rupees a day except on days when it rained heavily. With this and the irregular money received from the son-in-law, the three of us were somehow able to manage our food and the educational expenditure of my grandson,' said Kusum in her peculiar, husky voice. Things became worse when her son-in-law began loathing her presence on his infrequent visits. For each and everything that went wrong, trivial things like the wife's delay in providing him with a dry towel for his bath or his child getting beaten in a childhood brawl, he started blaming Kusum. On one of his visits, he declared that when he came the next time, he did not want to see his mother-in-law in his house.

Knowing Kusum for the last one year, I fail to understand how this well-mannered, genial, meek and gentle woman, who is incapable of uttering any word that can be termed as irritating or harsh, became the target of her son-in-law's wrath.

However, misfortune, for some, is like the fangs of a hydra-headed monster. It targets vulnerables mercilessly, and then strikes repeatedly. Once the pain inflicted by its venom reduces over time, the other head strikes with enhanced fury, until the victim becomes immune to pain.

In Kusum's case, her story narrated above gives an account of how misfortunes came her way one after another. After a brief lull, the monster targeted her again. First, her brother suffered a stroke and lost his locomotive ability. With four mouths to feed, her sister-in-law was at sea. Kusum could not seek shelter with them. Next was her back. It almost incapacitated her. Last was the intransigence of her son-in-law.

Kusum lingered on in her daughter's home for a while until the daughter begged her to leave them to save whatever little relationship she still had with her husband.

Kusum obliged. One evening, she decided not to return from the day's work of sitting and begging in front of the temple. When night fell, and darkness enveloped her, she lay sprawled on the roadside. It was winter and the chill was killing, sapping whatever remained of her will to live and survive.

She does not remember how she landed up in a street corner by the side of a busy crossroad. However, she does remember someone throwing her crumbs to eat and giving her water to drink. Some young girls, training to be nurses in the nearby hospital, noticed her lying on the roadside and asked her why she did not go home. She told them she lived with her daughter, but the daughter was unable to accommodate her further. She refused to divulge the address. They went away, hoping her daughter will come calling by evening. It was a weekend. On the next working day, when they came to the hospital, they found her lying almost immobile at the same place. After the day's work, they returned to her, made her sit up, and gave her some food. Then, they rang us up for help.

We rushed to the spot and brought her to Seneh. It was 18 June 2019. First she was given a hot bath and clean clothes to wear. Then some nourishment. She looked presentable. Luckily, a thorough medical check-up did not reveal any serious ailments other than Vitamin D deficiency and low calcium level. Honestly, she is an exception. Almost all the thirty-odd destitute we have accommodated in our home have had a range of ailments, both physical and mental. Some needed immediate hospitalisation. But for Kusum, the frail, short, seventy-year-old, it was a different story. With Vitamin D and calcium supplement for about two months, her back problem vanished. She became energetic and vibrant like a forty-year-old. Her physical appearance improved. Today she looks like a rose that has emerged from its bud.

Kusum is a darling with her egg-shaped face, long black hair with its few white streaks. She ties her hair together in a round, shining bun, the shine due to generous application of hair oil. Her skin has a dusky texture with splashes of blurred red as if the last rays of the setting sun had spilled over her face. Her skin remains taut and firm. There are no signs of wrinkles. Another feature of her radiant face is her perfectly shaped eyebrows that will shame any modern young lady. Her small eyes are bright and shining grey, like that of a kitten. The most striking feature of her small face is her aquiline nose, long and sharp at the end. Her signature toothless grin never leaves her face these days; the muscles around her lips contract, making a deep gorge around her mouth where the missing teeth existed.

Endowed with robust health, in the last two years, she has never fallen ill. Slightly bent forward in the middle, like the end of a bamboo tree, she has a peculiar walk. It appears she drags her unwilling left leg. Probably, when the brain commands the legs to move, the right leg complies immediately. The left does not react fast.

Her radiant smile, reflected in the brightness of her eyes, tells it all that she has ultimately found peace and tranquillity. Her daughter never inquired about her, leave alone visited her. Initially, she expected the daughter would come. When she did not, she accepted it as a decree of fate. She never displayed any disappointment. In the early days, when I asked her about her past, she was reluctant to respond. She told me, in a matter-of-fact tone, 'Please do not ask. I have left my past behind when I came here.' When I divulged my purpose, she relented.

Kusum is undoubtedly an angel. She never complains about anything. She never raised any issues about other co-residents of Seneh. That itself is unique, since quite often, our support staff is kept busy settling squabbles

Vivian

On A Train Away From Home

The cuckoos with their melodious voices were heralding good tidings. Spring was round the corner and was getting ready to knock at the door. As winter receded, the gentle cool breeze, *falguni*, began blowing its soothing spray on the body and mind. There was romance in the air. It was mid-March.

The grey bark of the mahua tree with its signature cracks, stood tall and imposing. It had shed its long leaves. The gnarled, naked, tender branches danced rhythmically, like village damsels dancing the *Jhumar*.

Manual Ingly, hollow-eyed, with an unevenly trimmed grey beard sprouting like the spikes of a runner's shoe on his face, watched the new buds that hung by the dozens from the ends of the branches of the mahua tree. A few tender leaves peeped from the puckered, naked branches besides the abundant flower buds. Involuntarily, his tongue licked his large lips. It would be days before the flowers would be in full bloom turning into the succulent musky flowers that his wife Mariam would use to make the local sweet brew, also called mahua. He loved his drinks and always wondered why the priest in his sermons urged church-goers to desist from drinking mahua or any other intoxicant. Didn't the Supreme Being, the God of all gods, Jesus Christ, himself partake glasses of wine, as shown in the famous painting, *Last Supper*, a replica of which hung on the church wall?

Situated downhill, on an undulated piece of land in the parched Chhotanagpur plateau of India, lay Manual's village. The nearest town was almost a day's trek away in mainland Bihar. Manual's hamlet comprised of roughly sixty-eight houses, all belonging to the prominent Munda community of Jharkhand state. Rich foliage of the gorgeous Sal (*Shorea Robusta*), Khair (*Acrosia Coreariu*), Arer (*Accosia Pinnala*) and the flowering mahua and *palash* trees surrounded the village. Occasionally, wild animals, mainly wild boar and barking deer would pay a fleeting, sudden, visit to the hamlet. At times, after nightfall, the deadly leopard also emerged, lifting a calf or a domestic pig as a prized catch. The village would wake up to commotion. The next morning, the children crowded around the pug marks. For the next couple of days, even the sudden appearance of a domestic dog scared the children when the long shadows of the evenings were engulfed by darkness. For weeks, they never ventured out alone after dark. The passage of time lifted the scare, like fog lifts when the sun peeks.

Manual's house, made of bamboo walls and a corrugated iron roof, was inadequate for his six offsprings and wife. Space was scarce and at night, all the young siblings slept together on the ground, on two mats spread together, packed like sardines. The parents shared a cot on the veranda, a soiled and torn mosquito net hanging over them. When their daughter Vivian and her elder brother grew up, another small room with a palm leaf roof was added.

They had a reasonably large piece of cultivable land to till for harvesting the paddy. The harvesting season started in the month of February and lasted until April. The rich land produced enough grain for the family of eight.

Sundays were special. All those who could make the one-hour trek to the church would set off in their best attire for the weekly congregation. Either her mother or Vivian was required to stay back to look after the youngest three, two toddlers and an infant. When she was around nine, young Vivian often officiated for her mother in rearing the young ones both during the cultivating seasons and on some Sundays.

'When I was ten, my elder brother died of diarrhoea,' Vivian said. 'He was so dear to me. He would go and fetch me succulent wild berries from the jungles to eat and wild orchid flowers to wear in my hair.' Even now, although she is around sixty-five, her eyes become moist when she remembers her elder brother. 'He used to climb like a simian on the trunk and the branches of the mahua trees to get the flowers for my mother to brew the wine,' she recalled. 'His tanned dark body glittered like sunrays, like the eyes of a cat when seen at night,' she added.

In their village, the death of a child at an early age was common and accepted in a matter-of-fact manner. Malnutrition, lack of hygiene, and no medical help were the main reasons. Thirty to forty per cent of the children died early. Age-old herbal medications and even black magic performed by sorcerers to drive out the evil spirit seldom saved an ailing child.

In addition to her elder brother, two of her four younger brothers also succumbed to ailments in the course of four years. Her father accepted it with stoic silence, like a log of deadwood on the ground that accepts both torrential rains or the heat of the scorching sun with the same stoicism.

'Life and death are God's balancing acts and are inevitable,' he argued. He believed that the balance was maintained in such a way that births still outnumbered deaths, ensuring not only the survival of their clan but also ensuring that the tribe flourishes.

The inevitability which he accepted as a matter of God's will, did not spare him either, for it robbed him of his life a year or so thereafter.

At fifteen, Vivian grew to be a charming, bubbly, hardy young woman. Her wavy long hair, black and shining because of regular use of mustard oil, grew evenly from her melon-shaped head. She had high cheekbones, slightly slanting eyes, a large flat nose, heavy lips and a perfect set of white, shiny teeth. The somewhat plump and well-developed body was generously proportioned and her light copper-coloured shining skin, taut and unblemished, exuded an aura of sensuality and energy.

It was Christmas eve mass in the church. She along with her family trekked the hour-long distance to attend the mass. She was wearing her best red-bordered white sari with a matching red *choli* (blouse). Her hair was bound into a bun behind her head and above her neck. She wore a long stranded orchid flower bunch over the bun. The knee-length sari revealed the lower portion of her long and strong legs. A silver ring with a small stone pendant adorned both the little fingers of her feet. With a red, round *bindi* and *godnas* (tattoos) on the back of her palms and a bigger one on the back of her neck, she looked superbly attractive and charming.

As if providence had ordained it, they sat on the end of two adjoining pews. She was sitting on the left pew, he on the right one. According to the rules of the Church, the men and women sat on separate sides of the church. The twenty-something Jewel Munda, from a nearby village, could not tear his eyes away from her and was unable to concentrate on his prayers. They rubbed each other's shoulders, she involuntarily, he by design, on the aisle of the church while leaving. His eyes never left her back when they took their different routes to their respective villages after a half-hour trek together.

One day, Jewel's sister visited Vivian's village, met her alone and begged her to meet her brother at least once in a secluded place. They met and the meetings became frequent. He proposed, she accepted, and finally, the parents exchanged pleasantries. About a year later, they were betrothed in a simple ceremony in the church; Vivian was seventeen and Jewel twenty-one.

Jewel was a healthy, relatively tall handsome man with a muscular, athletic body and a penchant for playing the flute. At night, after dinner, for an hour or so, he played his flute with rapt devotion, while Vivian finished her household chores, then settled down to listen to him.

Jewel lived with his parents. His unmarried sister and his elder brother along with his wife and two kids, also lived under the same roof. Lots of household responsibilities fell on Vivian's young shoulders. She was busy the whole day but never complained. However, making her mother-in-law happy was a tall order. She always found fault and harshly admonished the two daughters-in-laws, especially, Vivian.

Ten months later, Vivian conceived. Jewel had hardly any earnings. The family's survival depended on the farm produce of their paltry land holdings and the elder brother's business of selling small knick-knacks at the weekly markets in nearby villages. He carted his wares on a cycle with four big bags full of merchandise or in a bullock cart. In spite of persuasions, admonitions, and threats, Jewel abhorred the idea of selling goods. He hated standing the whole day guarding the merchandise spread in the bazaar on a piece of tarpaulin, and heckling with customers for a fair price for the items. The only occasion when he willingly participated in his brother's business was when both of them went shopping to buy their stock on a hired bullock cart to a nearby town. There was a thrill in it, especially the outward journey, when he would sit on the cart and play his tunes on his flute while crossing a wooded area or resting under a tree near a brook.

However, he was always ready to help his father on the farm. He also tended to their vegetable garden that yielded enough to cater to the family's needs. His best pastime was to dress neatly, tie his signature red scarf around his neck, smear his face with cheap talcum and then loaf around in their village laughing and joking with his friends. At times, he came back a little tipsy but he knew his limits and never crossed it.

Vivian was happy. She worked hard, slept well, and soothed her tired body listening to his flute at night. Jewel gave her all the tender love and affection a young wife deserved. The mother- and sister-in-law were hard to please, but she considered them as mere thorns that one encounters in the journey of life.

When she was just three months pregnant, Jewel surprised them all by announcing that along with two of his friends, he was leaving for Punjab to work as a farm labourer. A man on vacation from Punjab had informed them that there were plenty of jobs on the farms. He said that they would be able to earn three to four times more than what a farm labourer gets in their locality.

Everyone in the family welcomed his decision except Vivian. She wanted her husband by her side when she gave birth to their first child. She had dreamt of both of them bringing up their child together.

Jewel left. Vivian wept. She felt very lonely. At night, she missed Jewel's loving caresses, his manly odour, his reassuring presence.

Their son Anthony was born six months after his departure. She exchanged messages about their well-being through others but alas, Jewel never came home for a long time. A month before the delivery, her mother had taken her home. After the delivery, she developed a nagging, unexplained pain on the left side of her waist. She tried everything such as massages, herbal balms, even some allopathic medications prescribed by the quack who practised medicine in a nearby village; she even tried the sorcerer's remedies to drive away the evil spirit that had entered her body causing the pain. It was of no avail.

When Anthony was six months old, she went back to her in-laws. In horror and disbelief, she noticed the change in their attitude towards her. The worst was the way her elder sister-in-law behaved with her. They made her work through the day until late evening with her child tied to her back. She did all the household chores including sweeping, swabbing, washing clothes and utensils and even attended to the calls of nature of her sick father-in-law. Even the slightest slip brought about severe reprimands. And all this while she was still suffering from the unexplained back pain. The weight of the child tied to her back had worsened her sufferings. To make matters worse, her mother-in-law began beating her physically if she made any mistake.

Vivian was devastated. The chronic pain had affected her posture. Her husband did not come back—not once during the three years she lived with her in-laws. Then, one day, when she could bear it no longer, she walked off, carrying whatever clothes she could pack, and with her young son Anthony, who was little over three, on her back. She went back to her mother's place.

Life was tough there also. Her back pain was a constant discomfort. Her mother, who was now looking like a dried-up brinjal, withered and bent, lived a difficult life of suffering. Only her ten-year-old youngest brother lived with the mother. Her other brother had gone to a distant place and did not care for his mother. He even stopped communicating. Her sister lived with her husband and a baby far away. Her mother, out of dire need, sold off half of the cultivable land they had.

Vivian was determined to make a successful man out of Anthony so that he would not have to suffer the humiliations and neglect she had suffered in her life. In spite of her physical deformity (by then, she could not stand straight), she resolved to work hard, not only in their own field but also in others'. Luckily, other than the deformity, her health was robust. She was capable enough to do strenuous work. Every night, after her son slept, her tired body yearned for rest. When asleep, she dreamt of ghosts and serpents, of human excreta and filth, her mother-in-law lashing her, her sister-in-law tormenting her.

Then, one fine day, when Anthony was five, her husband turned up laden with plenty of gifts for their son and new saris for her. Initially, Anthony was resentful for what he clearly regarded as an unwelcome intrusion into their lives. His mother's loving attention to Jewel infuriated him but within days, the father and son became inseparable. Vivian was elated.

Jewel took his family back home. The old

belligerence between the mild and submissive Vivian and the mercurial acid-tongued mother- and daughter-in-law duo miraculously disappeared. Anthony became the apple of his grandmother's eyes, much to the chagrin of his aunt.

The bonhomie and truce continued for two years until Jewel departed, once again, for Punjab. The old animosity reappeared, slowly but even more resolutely, like poisonous mushrooms sprouting out of a decaying, long-dead tree trunk.

Anthony started going to school. For his sake, she silently bore all the humiliation. She worked tirelessly to placate her mother-in-law.

Jewel came home a couple of times and spent a month or two with them. He spent half his time with his old friends and acquaintances.

When he was around, relative peace and tranquillity prevailed. But it was always the proverbial lull before a storm. For, within days after Jewel's departure, the storm lashed her again in full fury, like high-speed winds that make the trees shudder and sway. She withstood the fury of the winds in silence, knowing fully well that her protests will bring more belligerence. At times, the domestic cyclone left her battered with injuries, some of them inflicted by her brother-in-law.

In all fairness to her brother-in-law, such incidents were few. He was, basically, a good, peace-loving, sensible man who was scared of his wife. If he protested at the injustice towards Vivian, his wife, in a fit of rage, targeted their three children and Anthony with a vengeance. He knew the only way he could placate her was to use strong-arm tactics against his helpless sister-in-law. As a consequence, it was poor Vivian who bore the brunt.

'Sir, I withstood all that ignominy without a whimper because of Anthony. Gradually, I gave up on my husband. Whenever he came home, he would spend more time outside home and one day, on his way back from school, Anthony saw him in the house of a single woman. On enquiry, I found that Jewel was seeing her regularly.'

This devastated her completely. The mental torture she went through because of his infidelity was far worse than the physical torture she was going through.

'I decided for the sake of my son that I will bear everything silently. I could have started living with my sister, who always invited me with Anthony, to come and stay with her permanently. But there was no high school within a 5-km radius. Anthony's schooling was more important to me than my own self-respect,' she said.

Jewel now started coming home every six months. Vivian had started looking old, what with her bent back and the mental and physical tortures she was undergoing. Perhaps that was the reason why Jewel found her unattractive. Her over-zealous obsession with her son

Anthony was another irritant.

Vivian says that she tried very hard to please Jewel. But his response was always cold. 'I went through hell,' Vivian lamented.

Worse was yet to come. One fine evening, Jewel brought home the much younger woman he was seeing. Vivian was aghast when she learnt that her mother-and sisters-in-law encouraged him to bring the woman home. He did not marry her as the church never sanctions bigamy. Their culture disapproved of divorce.

Simple, kind-hearted Vivian willingly offered her bed to them and took refuge in an outhouse that stank of cow urine and dung.

'In those troubling times, God gave me strength. The church was my saviour,' she said. When the parish priest read aloud Psalm 40:1-3 in their native language: 'God is our refuge and strength, an ever-present help in trouble' or Psalm 9: 9-10: 'The Lord is a refuge for the oppressed, a stronghold in times of trouble,' she found solace and peace.

'One day, while in church, I discovered Jesus Christ the saviour hath entered my body. I started shaking involuntarily,' explained Vivian when we asked her the reason for her trances that we have been noticing, every time she went to the Church or sometimes when offering the all-religion prayers chanted at Seneh.

When Anthony was about sixteen years old and was preparing for his matriculation exam, Vivian made it a point to sit with him until late at night to give him company while he was studying, although she did not even know the alphabets. She ensured that the best of nourishment and comfort was available to him. Unfortunately, all her hopes were shattered when the results were announced. He failed. That ended his studies. He started loafing around with friends in the village. She also heard complaints of his passing lewd remarks about the village girls.

She persuaded him to start working and after a lot of haggling and cajoling, he left for a town in a nearby province to find work, which he eventually did. On her part, she decided to leave her in-laws and shift to her sister's place, a three hour' journey on foot.

Her sister was relatively well off and the brother-in-law was genial. The sister wanted her help to bring up her three children, all born two years apart from each other. Vivian was happy. She enjoyed the company of the children. But, at times, she longed to be independent and not be a burden on the family. In a couple of months, her son came to visit and left some money with her, promising to visit again within the next one year. He said he would be back and would construct a small cottage where his mother could live comfortably.

She waited for him but he never came for more than two years. On the contrary, she heard that he had been visiting his father. That was like sprinkling salt on her wounds. Even her own son, for whom she had withstood so much humiliation and contempt, had chosen to ignore her deliberately. For the first time in her life, Vivian, who never complained, decided to confront and demand an explanation first from him, and then from God.

She walked to her husband's house. She had heard that Anthony was going to be there on a holiday. Her heart told her that he would never betray her trust and love. She promised her sister that she would certainly return—with Anthony in tow. She trudged the distance non-stop unmindful of the pain in her back. When she finally reached, she was told Anthony had left for his workplace two days back. Her husband, too, had left for Punjab. Her mother-in-law and brother-in-law were quite cordial. She spent the night there, and next morning, before the others awoke, she left for the church. She met the priest and told him her tale of woe. He listened, then read aloud a passage from Psalm 9:9 1: 'The Lord is a refuge for the oppressed, a stronghold in times of trouble.'

He advised her to be patient and seek solace in the altar of the Lord with devotion and belief. She emerged from the church unconvinced that this was the only way forward. Then she did the unthinkable.

Armed with a stick and a small packet of clothes and with just Rs 35, she started walking, like a possessed woman, towards the state border, to go to the place where

Anthony worked. He had told her earlier that the town's name was Bhawanipur. To reach the place, one needed to take the train to Rourkela, famous for its steel plant, and then press further by bus.

After walking for five hours, she reached the main road and stopped a bus. When asked for her destination and fare, she told the conductor that she wanted to go to Rourkela. He said the bus would take her to the railway station from where she could board a train for her destination.

At the railway station, she was awed by the size of the train and by the number of people travelling in it. People were hanging from the coaches like bees clustering on hives.

Without knowing the route of the train that was about to leave the station, she managed to board a crowded coach and found a place to stand. She travelled like that overnight. The train stopped at various stations where some people disembarked. The crowd thinned and finally, she found a place to rest and dozed off.

She was shaken awake by a rough hand that belonged to an unkempt, bearded stranger. The train had reached its destination. The stranger, a beggar, pulled her out of the compartment, just in time before the train started moving to the yard. The bearded beggar, hollow-eyed, thin, and in rags, looked at her disdainfully. 'One more competitor in my trade,' he must have thought, before walking away.

'Till date, I do not know what place was that. I only remember that with a part of the money I had, I bought something to eat. Then I saw a train stopping, and without bothering to know where it was heading, I boarded it. No one asked me for my destination or for my ticket. When the train reached its destination, after a long ride, I was the last to alight. I was tired and hungry. I still had some money, so I ate, then fell asleep in one corner of the platform.

'I do not remember if I woke up on my own in the morning or if someone shook me awake. I found myself in an alien place where people spoke a language I did not understand. Lots of people were loitering there, old and young, some in rags. Well-dressed people went by, some in a hurry and others walking leisurely carrying bags. In some cases, they were followed laboriously by red-shirted coolies carrying heavy loads on their heads,' said Vivian.

'After a while, I noticed a young boy, his face smeared with dirt, his clothes in tatters and asked him in Hindi the name of the place where she was.' She was in Guwahati.

The boy had a hearty laugh when she told him in Hindi how she had landed up there. He then told her that he himself was a wanderer like her. He had no parents or relations. Noticing Vivian's helplessness, he promised to help. He led her to a place under the railway over-bridge where he lived with scores of others of all ages. He gave her a few slices of stale bread, asked her to take rest, and disappeared to return late at night. Later, she learnt that he begged and also did rag-picking. He introduced her to these professions.

With his help, she found a vacant place below the bridge, made a bed with some dry leaves and started a new life. Open defecation on the tracks and a bath under the pipe used for refilling the bathrooms of the coaches were the norms that every inhabitant who lived there, followed.

She gradually started following them. She took to begging and barely made money to buy herself a meal. She also scavenged for leftovers from passengers' food plates. On some lucky days, she could afford to buy herself a second meal and a cup of tea.

In a month's time, she had saved some money to buy a dirty bedspread from one of her cohabitants for use at night. She started collecting discarded plastic water bottles so that she could sell them later to buy a blanket for the approaching winters.

After a month's effort, her treasure trove of empty bottles had swelled. She did a quick calculation. Possibly, with the sale of this collection, she would be able to buy a blanket and a new saree. She planned that in a few months, she would have the capability to pay for her way back home.

She walked off towards the city to find a recyclable plastic dealer. When she came back with a handcart to carry her bounty back to the dealer, she heard that in her absence, some vagabonds and drug addicts living on the platform had made away with her treasure. That was the last straw.

The sky fell on her. She lost her bearings, as if the compass in her brain stopped working abruptly.

***

Vivian was lying by the side of a hilly track, 5-6 km from the railhead in a dishevelled and completely disoriented state. She was so weak that she was unable to even stand or open her eyes. Some youngsters spotted her and informed us about an old woman in dirty, soiled clothing lying unconscious by the side of the mud road. Our volunteers immediately sprang into action. They found her there and informed the nearby police station. Promptly, the police picked her up along with our representatives and brought her to Seneh. They completed all the legal formalities, made us sign some papers and then left her under our care. The first thing our caretaker did was to summon the doctor, clean her up, gave her a cup of tea with a few biscuits. She devoured it in no time.

The doctor said she was weak due to hunger, thirst and exhaustion. He administered medicated drips. In an hour, she was able to sit unassisted. Thereafter, she ate a hearty meal with ravenous urgency and zeal. After some time, with absolutely bewildered and lost eyes, she enquired about her whereabouts in Hindi. Recognising the compassionate and friendly eyes of our team, she gave a wry smile. She was then assisted to have a thorough hot bath, and was given new clothes to wear. She collected her bedding, made her bed in the appointed place, and slept immediately, seemingly calm and content.

A somewhat hard nudge woke her up the next morning. She had to be taught first how to use the toilet and clean it after use, and, also how to use a toothbrush. Afterwards, she sat, with unblinking eyes and rapt devotion, when the others said their ritualistic community morning prayers. Prayers done, she joined the others for breakfast. Later, she was given a close-cropped haircut, somewhat haphazardly by a nurse who had no experience. Subsequently she had a cold bath. After donning clean clothes, she ate breakfast. With a sense of trust in her mind, she looked comfortable and radiant.

Thus on 27 April 2018, Vivian became a resident of Seneh. I have noticed remarkable and astonishing adaptability in this simple tribal woman of Jharkhand. In a matter of months, she has adjusted well to the predominant Assamese culture of the other inhabitants, taken to their dressing pattern, habits, cultural ethos and food habits. She now joins the others in all activities as part of the team, and is able to understand every word spoken in Assamese. She communicates with others in a mixed language of Assamese, Hindi and her own dialect.

With her peculiar gait of curving rightward with the left hip projecting outward, probably because of permanent disfigurement of her back, it is a riveting scene to look at her dancing along with the others, the immensely popular folk dance of Assam, the Bihu. She also takes part in the Assamese chorus that the residents sing as the signature song of Seneh during all festivities. She always has a smile on her lips when she talks to the other inmates, and constantly gives a toothless grin of a woman, finally satisfied with a life of relative comfort, dignity and camaraderie and the experience of feeling wanted.

In the morning and evening prayers, the residents sing together a prayer taught to all by the nuns of the local church praising Lord Jesus, the all-merciful along with Hindu hymns. Every time the Christian prayer is said, Vivian automatically goes into a catalcptic state, as if in a stupor, and starts shaking involuntarily with closed eyes. Anyone who sees her in this state for the first time is bound to think she is going off the rails but within minutes of completing the prayer, Vivian turns back into her normal self, radiating energy and exuberance.

Vivian is a healthy woman. She has not fallen sick even once in the last three years except for toothaches that necessitated extraction of her two incisors. In the first COVID wave, all the residents excepting Vivian and

Sarala tested positive. All came out unscratched.

Author's Note: Vivian's story is based on the account she gave me in several one-on-one sessions. My efforts to give her story a real-life image, based on her accounts, is a product of my imagination and understanding. I did research about the culture, habits and social lives of the Mundas, the community to which she belongs. I studied the flora and fauna of their habitat, but any error in describing her life is solely a result of my ignorance, and for that, I tender an apology. Honestly, this statement is true for all the characters, living or dead, whose lives I have portrayed in this book.

I also want to inform the readers, that we made an honest effort to trace her son Anthony. We wrote to her district's police head with whatever information about him that we could extract from her, to help us locate him. We drew a blank. We would have been immensely happy if we could have united mother and son, even if only for a short while.

As for Vivian, she gives an impression, she has buried her past and is living happily in her present. The ever-present smile and radiance on her face tell it all.

Somari Orang

Happiest By Herself

DHIN DI NA DHIN, DA DIDA DA DHIN, the rhythmic sound of the *madal* (a long wooden drum, with a bulging middle, both ends covered with taut calf leather, and played by both hands) and the soft, soothing sound of the flute pervaded the quiet moonlit evening in Somari's hamlet. As the sound reverberated over the waist-high, neatly manicured tea groves that separated the hamlet from the open green area, Somari involuntarily responded to the beats, her heart pounding. April had arrived and with it the *kopou* flowers, a type of parasitic orchid which hangs long like an elegant necklace from the mother tree. The tender tea leaves danced, swaying sideways, cajoled by the gentle breeze, as if the rhythm of the drumbeats was the reason for the breeze luring the leaves.

She could not contain herself. She trotted off limping, dragging her polio-affected left leg to the spot where she was sure to find the older girls and boys dancing in unison, in a ring with the two drummers and the bansuri players in the centre. The dancers had formed a circle, a boy followed by a girl, holding each other's waists with their hands. The dance required intricate footwork, with feet thumping in unison, moving to the right with every step and bending bodies forward and backward with each step. The Zhumur dance is a signature dance of the tea tribes, who are descendants of tribals and backward classes brought by the colonial tea planters of Britain as indentured labour in the middle of the nineteenth century to work in the tea gardens. They are from the Chhotanagpur plateau of present-day Jharkhand, Chhattisgarh, Odisha, West Bengal and Telangana. Initially, they lived in ghettoes and were not allowed to mix with the native Assamese community of the area.

Most of the Assamese followed the teachings of the sixteenth century Vaishnavite teacher Srimonta Sankaradeva and embraced religiosity and righteousness over materialistic pursuits. They, therefore, refused to work as labourers. The colonial masters wanted to insulate the tea labourers they had brought in from the local Assamese, and so made them live in segregated areas, which ensured they did not come in contact with the locals. They also cut off all escape routes. They were denied any access to education. Their only relief from the rigours of daily back-breaking work was the heady brew they were surreptitiously encouraged to drink. Both sexes liked their booze.

Although this is a digression from the story of Somari, I would like to relate a personal experience of how the fair-skinned managers of the tea gardens ruled. Five years after independence, along with my parents, I visited a tea garden where one of my uncles worked. It was a time when British managers were still around. The *Burra Sahib* (chief manager), and his two assistant Chhota Sahibs were all British. They lived in sprawling bungalows with dozens of servants, all tea labourers, at their beck and call. Other than the servants, no other labourer was allowed to even walk down the main road as the bungalows stood by the side of the road.

The labourers were forced to take a long detour to avoid passing by the bungalows. The other brown administrative staff such as clerks, factory assistants, work supervisors and medical staff were allowed on the road with certain restrictions. If a person from this category rode a bicycle, they had to alight and walk across dragging their cycles when crossing the bungalows. Looking at the bungalow directly was forbidden. If a man had an open umbrella on his head, he was to close it irrespective of the weather while crossing the stretch.

The assistant managers walked the mud road separating rows of tea plantations to supervise with a long whipping lash in their hands to punish the labourers for the slightest dereliction of duty. Looking straight into the eyes of the managers was considered an act of insubordination. It resulted in lashes.

Coming back to Somari's story, all the dancers and drummers were high on the heady country liquor purchased from the makeshift shop that operated from under the banyan tree that stood in a corner of the field.

Somari was thirteen. She had sharp features, an elongated nose, protruding small eyes and striking bushy eyebrows. Her taut skin was unblemished, her hair curly and jet black, and her pout mesmerising. Looking at her, no one could imagine the lightly built charming girl not only had a polio-affected leg with weak muscles, she was also mentally under-developed for her age and had a slight stammer.

Buddu and Guddu, her two elder brothers, were part of the dancing group, along with her elder sister Champa. She could spot Chameli, the vivacious sweetheart of her eldest brother Buddu, holding his waist with her left hand while she held the waist of Chandu, another of her admirers, with her right hand. Chameli was a graceful, energetic dancer, certainly the best dancer in the crowd. She also had the swiftest pair of hands and plucked almost twice the quantity of tender tea leaves than the other labourers in a day. Every morning, in the plucking season, the men and women filed into the tea gardens in neat rows with baskets hanging from their heads. The others were employed to maintain the groves and clean the pathways between the groves.

With her healthy leg tapping, the neck swaying in rhythm, and heart pounding in thrill, Somari was lost in the vigour of the dance until a drunken brawl between two of the male dancers broke up the merrymaking. The brawl escalated into fisticuffs and Somari ran back home with other children in panic. Her mother received her with mock anger for going to watch the dance without her knowledge.

Her mother, over sixty and in poor health, always treated her with kid gloves. The average longevity of the tea tribes is fifty-two against the national average of sixty-seven today. She walked with a supporting stick. Her husband had died a few years back leaving her with five children of varying ages to look after, three elder to Somari and a boy two years her junior.

Somari was slow and unintelligent. The other children shunned and mocked her. The elders always chased away those who tried to belittle her but children can be cruel to each other. They enjoyed irritating Somari and made her shed many tears. As she grew, she became morose and withdrawn. She preferred being alone doing nothing. The mother tried to involve her in housekeeping jobs like sweeping, swabbing, washing clothes, chopping vegetables and when Somari was twelve, involving her in cooking. But she never displayed interest in anything. She took twice the time others take to sweep the small two-room hut they lived in. Her cooking was always a disaster. Sometimes, she would forget to add salt to the dish or would end up adding salt twice. Her friends called her *Bengeri*, meaning the one who was mentally differently abled. Honestly, her disability was not that serious to warrant such a sobriquet. She felt hurt and wept, often secretly.

She keenly waited for the Karam festival celebrated each year on the eleventh day of the moon phase of Bhadra (August-September). The festival entails worshipping the karam tree. The tea tribes believe the karam tree is a symbol of fertility and wealth. Nine days before the actual festival, the villagers pack nine varieties of grain in baskets and hand them over to an unmarried maiden, who is required to tend to them. The basket aggregate is called *jawa.* For four years in a row, Somari was the maiden selected to look after the *jawa.* It was an honour and Somari looked forward to the importance and honour she got in the process, little knowing, that the elders conferred on her this privilege out of pity and not due to any other considerations.

The festival took off with the villagers going to the

nearby forest to collect a healthy branch of a karam tree and plant it in the middle of the open field. The priest offered puja to the branch. Thereafter, the *jawa*s were brought on the heads of nine girls, in a procession, with Somari in the lead, for the worshipping ritual. The daylong festivities included group dancing and feasting. Three roosters were sacrificed to please the deity, the revered karam tree. In addition, a cock fight was organised, as a pastime, during the festival.

For the fight, the contestants, two owners, bring a healthy cock each. They tie small pieces of shaving blades to their paws. The cocks are let loose and instigated to fight. They fight tooth and nail, until one of them drops dead because of exhaustion and heavy bleeding. The owner of the winning cock takes a hefty collection from the onlookers. Cock fights are common in all tea tribe-dominated areas even today.

***

When Somari was seventeen, her mother died. By then, her eldest brother was married to Chameli. After a few years, the couple migrated to an unknown place with their two children, never to return home. When she was around thirty, her other brother also left his job in the tea garden and cleared an area of government-owned forest land together with seven of his friends. Each one occupied half an acre of the land, constructed a hut and shifted there with their families. Her brother took Somari along. Gradually, as more people joined in, a decent hamlet evolved, where they tilled the land and reared their goats and poultry, thus making a living. They also brought with them the vibrant culture of the tea tribes.

Somari helped her brother in the cultivation of the land and took good care of the pets. With time, her brother had to feed bigger mouths as his four children grew. On the other hand, the yield became less. To augment the earnings of the family, Somari and her sister-in-law worked in the nearby quarry to break stones. For a day's hard work, her sister-in-law earned rupees thirty a day. Since Somari was weak and habitually slow, she earned half this amount.

Then, an unprecedented drought caused serious crop failure. To add to the family's miseries, her brother fell ill. She now became a huge burden to the family. In order of priority, she was the last to get food. She got weaker by the day.

Her younger brother, a gardener at Guwahati, had three children to look after. To boost their income, his wife worked as an assistant in a nursery school. The brother brought Somari to look after the children when his wife was away. But the differently abled was more of a liability rather than a help to the family. In all fairness, her sister-in-law always understood and tried her best to be nice to Somari. Eventually, it was she who came to Seneh requesting help. She frankly explained to us in great detail Somari's mental and physical state. Her honesty and sincerity impressed us. We accepted Somari as a new resident in Seneh.

Somari joined the Seneh family on 2 September 2018. It was a warm sultry afternoon when Somari, led by her sister-in-law, walked limping to our office a thin, pale, hollow-eyed middle-aged woman dressed in tatters. She was shaking from head to toe, too scared to make any eye contact with us. She answered our queries reluctantly in a feeble voice. Her hair was tied at the back with several strands peering out that flew with the breeze of the ceiling fan. She looked under-nourished, pale and weak with parched lips and sunken eyes.

Somari has spent more than three years at Seneh. She has gained weight, her skin now glows and the hollow look in her eyes has disappeared. Above all, her gait has transformed: We were astonished to discover that she does not limp any more. Till date, she has not suffered from any ailment, save mild COVID infection. Her voice has gained a resonance. If someone asks her a question, she answers back politely, making firm eye contact. She does not stammer so much. She sits solemnly with closed eyes for the mandatory morning and evening prayers while keeping her lips locked. She takes part in all group activities with a sort of stoic resignation. Left alone, she seems happier, and abhors interacting with others. The psychiatrist said there is no cure for her aloofness since it is a sort of inferiority complex and has made a permanent dent on her psyche. But among all the capable old residents of Seneh, Somari is one of a select few who has never crossed words with anyone or complained about the others. She avoids enmity and has never had an argument with anyone. She is undoubtedly the most uncontroversial, disciplined, non-argumentative, peace-loving, quietest and perhaps the most introverted resident of Seneh. With her incisors gone, her smile is mesmerising.

Rahima

Living By Grace Of Allah

At the very outset, let me state that Rahima did not qualify to be a member of the Seneh family, because, she was, and still is, too young to be eligible. We do not provide shelter to women of less than fifty years of age. Rahima looked around forty when she became a member of the Seneh family. What made us break the rules then? In two words, the answer is: compulsion and compassion. It is triumph of humanitarian consideration over rules.

The next question that is likely to pop up in the minds of the readers could be: who was she before she arrived at Seneh and what were her antecedents? Our answer: 'We do not know.'

Was she able to talk when she came? Again a

resounding no. Then how did we know her name?

Rahima's story starts from these natural questions. The only leads about her origin or background she gave out were her protesting shrill shrieks that hit us like gunfire when our working team attempted to get rid of the immensely foul-smelling tuft of her knotted hair which was in total disarray. Also, as she squirmed and squealed when our nurses forcefully tended to her grievous wounds, she spat out loud and clear, two words that we could decipher as 'Ma Go' (Oh Ma) and 'Hai Allah'. We concluded that she or her family were originally from eastern Bangladesh (they have a distinct way of pronouncing words) and she is a Muslim by religion.

So, when the requirement for identifying her from the rest of the residents arose, one of our dedicated volunteers, a practising Muslim, named her Rahima, meaning 'Allah's *raham*' (the grace of Allah). We started calling her by that name and it remained her official identity. And today, she also responds to that name. There was no way of knowing her father's or mother's names, so on the official document we sent to the local police station, we wrote in broad letters: 'Not known.'

On a humid summer morning in the month of July 2019, when the weather was oppressive and venturing out required courage, our office received a call from a woman who said she was standing by the side of a heavily wounded woman lying unconscious under a busy flyover in a crowded area of Guwahati. She added that she had come to have a look at this woman after seeing a picture of her on a Facebook post uploaded a couple of hours back by someone. She requested help to take the woman to a hospital.

It took some time for our volunteers accompanied by a nurse to reach the spot. There was no one there. On inquiry, eyewitnesses informed our team that the wounded woman was taken away in a car by some young men. The team proceeded to the Guwahati Medical College hospital. That decision tilted the balance in favour of the wounded woman.

At the Emergency Ward of the hospital, they met the woman who called earlier. She turned out to be known to us, as she had been visiting Seneh. She informed them that since our team was late in reaching the spot, she had become apprehensive that the injured woman might not survive long and therefore she solicited help from some boys she knew. They picked up the woman's almost limp body, and brought her to the hospital half an hour back. But the busy emergency medical team was yet to attend to her. She requested our team to take over and then left.

Our team then managed a bed for her and since all the nurses of the hospital were busy, they tended to her wounds under the command of a trainee doctor. Later, a staff doctor joined them. The doctor opined that the woman, in all probability, was a hit-and-run victim, and said they were duty bound to inform the police. In the meanwhile, they started working on her treatment.

With active participation of our team, her wounds were cleaned and bandaged. She was administered some injections and intravenous fluids. In about an hour, the patient revived. On the advice of the doctors, our team arranged for a meal for her from the local market and fed her. She gulped it all down hungrily. Thereafter, an MRI of her head and a few x-rays were taken. Except for a few broken ribs, the injuries were all external. The police also came and said that since the patient was out of danger, we could take her to Seneh. Thus, Rahima was brought to Seneh in an ambulance provided by the hospital.

The first challenge was to clean her up. She was stinking like a country pig rescued from a scum-filled pit full of human excreta and decayed food. My choice of simile may offend some readers, but that was the first comparison that came to mind. I was a witness to the whole saga.

She had dried and caked human excreta embedded in her long, knotted hair. Her clothes stank of urine and vomit. The first priority was to cut her hair short. But it became a challenge, as she protested, howled and shrieked like a wounded animal when our volunteers approached her. It took four volunteers to restrain her.

According to the volunteers, her frail, bony body had tremendous strength. On my advice, our only male employee, a young Gurkha, was called in, to restrain her. A video of the operation is available on our website. Ultimately, her hair was cut. Washing her body was the next challenge, which was easier because her energy to resist had sapped by then. Cleaned up thoroughly and dressed in new clothes, she looked presentable.

But in all this, her bandages had got wet, and had to be changed. Once again, she protested and shrieked, but finally, the job was completed. Post-bandaging, she was given food. Her insatiable hunger astounded all and we had to stop her from eating too much. She had already eaten enough that would have sufficed three people. Next, she had to be taught the use of an English-style commode since bandages on her knee prevented her from using the Indian kind. Finally, she was put to bed. She slept for thirteen hours.

Next morning, she forgot the way to use the commode and had to be taught again. Later, for giving a bath, once again force was used. She used all her might to resist it. The next challenge was to make her wear fresh clothes. The entire staff of three ladies devoted their full efforts to make her wear a fresh set of clothes.

After breakfast, she was taken to a private hospital for consultation. The doctors were horrified to see the wound in one of her toes. Other injuries were bandaged, antibiotics prescribed, and a belt for supporting her broken ribs was donated by the hospital authorities.

In the doctor's opinion, the damaged toe was incurable. They advised us to bring her the next day for amputation of the toe. However, the head of Seneh's supporting staff decided to give regular dressing a try for a week. Three of them would pin her down every second day to dress her toe. One day, some neighbours came to inquire what was wrong when her shrill shrieks reached their ears.

The struggle continued with three tasks still difficult to negotiate: bathing, dressing her wounds and feeding. Her hunger was insatiable. She ate three times more than others and had to be physical stopped thereafter. Whenever she had a chance, she ate leftovers in the plates of the others. She became a big challenge to manage.

Our dedicated staff did not lose heart. Two factors were in their favour. First, the healing process was good and except for the lone injury on her toe, her other wounds were healing well. The other was the belt she was forced to wear around her waist that restrained her from picking up crumbs from the floor. Astonishingly, her toe started healing. It took forty-five days for it to heal completely. Her ribs joined. But her resistance to bathing and changing clothes continued, although the intensity began weakening.

We circulated her photograph to find out if anyone would come forward to identify her. A local TV channel also flashed her photograph. The next day, we were excited when we received a phone call when a caller claimed that Rahima was her lost daughter. We requested them to come immediately with proof. We also alerted the police. Two of them, a mother and her adult son, came the next day. Within minutes of meeting Rahima, the mother's eyes were moist with disappointment. Their daughter was taller, fairer and weighed more than Rahima. She positively was not their missing daughter. They went away crestfallen. No one else contacted us thereafter.

So Rahima stayed on. To sort out her mental afflictions, we sent her to a psychiatrist. He found her extremely difficult to manage. She not only refused to answer his questions but also had to be restrained from walking out from his chambers. Fortunately, she never displayed any tendency towards violence. The good doctor prescribed her oral medication and advised us to get her evaluated again after a month. The medication made her slow, subdued and less vociferous. Her insatiable appetite and urge for food also reduced substantially.

After a month, when she was taken again to the doctor, she cooperated without much fuss, though all his questions fell on deaf ears. Like a child, she kept concentrating on the objects on his table and played with the glass paper weight. The doctor gave his final verdict.

Rahima suffered from dual maladies. First was a deep-rooted psychological disorder which he would be able to manage partially with life-long medications.

But the other malady had no solution. Her brain cells were under-developed. Her mental development was comparable to that of a six-year-old.

She has been on psychiatric drugs for two years now which has subdued her. She has started getting up on her own in the mornings like the others, freshening up unassisted, and dressing up with fresh clothes, which she has learned to wash. She has also started sitting still on the prayer mat with the others, although not regularly, and eating her food quietly.

With a feeble voice, she normally requests more than her share of food. Beyond this, her behaviour is quite unpredictable. She requires constant watching, for at any moment, she may disappear. Earlier, she would scale the walls and the iron gate and go out stealthily. Thrice she had to be retrieved from the busy street, around 400 metres away, where she was wandering aimlessly. We have now devised ways to prevent her wayward behaviour. First, we keep the gates locked. Then, sharp iron spikes are welded on top of the gates. Secondly nails are embedded on the walls, so that she is unable to scale them.

She walks slowly and silently, often speaking in a thin, sparrow-like voice. When visitors come, unless prevented, she approaches them and begs for a portion of the snacks served with their tea. Like a child who has been taught some manners, she approaches each visitor with folded hands and expresses inaudible greetings. If one strains the ears, he or she may be able to catch her saying '*Namaskar*'. Her behaviour has improved vastly and she is positively no longer a nuisance. But she is still restless. She cannot sit or stand in one place for more than a few minutes. Strangely, during prayer time, she is a different person. With closed eyes, she listens to others saying their prayers, although she never utters any prayer, herself. Lately she has become more responsive and disciplined. She even started helping others in sundry jobs.

I must confess, when I imagine myself in her shoes, my own thoughts confuse me. Which life is better: Our so-called normal lives or should life be lived for today, the past and future not at all a matter of reminiscence or worry?

In Rahima's world, there is no joy in achievements or pain in failures. The world for her is like a small circle, and it is her exclusive domain. There is no lust, desire, enmity or friendship. Her only requirement in life is some food to survive. Her mind wanders aimlessly, like air, the direction and purpose not defined. Sometimes, she is happy at the smallest favour anyone does for her. The open sky is her world. She lives for today in a world where tomorrow has no relevance.

Try comparing it with the life that we live–one that is full of push, pull and contradictions, a life in which the lines between emotions and ego, between love and lust, between hatred and friendship, between compassion and motives, between responsibilities and self-interests, is always blurred.

EPILOGUE

The short, and at times, scanty biographies I have chosen to portray in the book, illustrate the malaise that plagues modern society today. The gradual erosion of values, lack of concern and empathy for the weak and the deprived, and the upholding of selfish motives in pursuing one's goals that often requires trampling by foot the fellow travellers in complete disregard of their physical and mental disabilities and afflictions—have unfortunately become the bane of modern society. Some of the women that I wrote about have found themselves abandoned purely because they trusted the wrong men or because they were married to men who fell prey to alcoholism.

Such happenings were relatively unknown in Indian society in yesteryears. With a solid family system, the weak and the sick, the old and the unfortunate were all comforted by their own families. They felt wanted and loved.

Luckily, a few level-headed and compassionate souls are showing concern for this section of society and are taking positive, firm and steady steps to help ameliorate the sufferings of these victims of ruthless circumstances. The government has also launched several welfare programmes and schemes to uplift this section of society but plenty still needs to be done.

A total of forty-four unfortunate old destitute women have got succour under the aegis of Seneh so far in the last ten years of its existence. Not all of them are living here now. A few have died and a few were reunited with their families. In choosing the women I have written about in this book, I went by certain basic tenets.

First, I took their consent and have profiled only the ones willing to be featured.

There are four exceptions.

There are a few whose own folly and ego landed them in this situation. I avoided them.

I studiously avoided those women who still have living relatives. I have no intention to ruffle, unnerve and shame these people. The only exception was the late Sadhana Borah. In her case, in exasperation, I had already published her story immediately after her death in a local daily.

Last, in a few cases, I found nothing pivotal to peg their stories or to explain how they landed up on the streets. In other words, I found hardly anything in their lives that would make a readable story.

In this epilogue, I am mentioning briefly the real

stories of two residents who are from the third category. I have taken care to keep their identities shrouded. One of Seneh's residents is accomplished, talented, level-headed, energetic and popular and although well over fifty, is still attractive and vivacious. When she was around forty, she fell for a dubious man two years younger to her. She misjudged deceit for empathy, lust for love and his dubious machinations for loyalty and honesty. Breaking all barriers, she legally separated from her scholarly, litterateur husband of twelve years, and her eight-year-old son, to start a life of love and bliss. She got cheated. He had merely used her as a mistress until he found another woman to marry. She was devastated, spurned all the largesse he offered and started living on her own, working as a semi-skilled labourer in a cycle factory. To drown her sorrows, she took to drinking. She was on the brink of destroying herself when a young man brought her to Seneh. She staggered in, a skeleton of a woman, stinking of cheap country liquor, slurring in an incoherent voice. We reluctantly accommodated her, weaned her away from drinking, provided treatment and professional psychiatric guidance, and today, she is the vibrant personality I described earlier. I have avoided penning her story as there may still be people who know her.

Then, there is the story of the late Lazzu (name changed). Hers is a story of man's wavering nature, cupidity and disloyalty. It brings tears to my eyes when

I remember her even today, long after her sad demise from stomach cancer, five and a half years ago. I do not remember having ever met a woman with her wisdom, level-headedness and the power to forgive and forget those who made her life a living hell. I was truly saddened when I once saw, with my own eyes, the way she had earlier lived all alone in a dingy basement room of a sprawling bungalow in downtown Guwahati.

Once upon a time, I was told, she even owned the land where the building stood. She sacrificed her life, her personal comfort and happiness for the sake of her two brothers. The three were orphaned when still in school. They inherited a good fortune. She remained a spinster for their sake, bringing up her younger siblings like a mother would. She gave up studies, although she was a brilliant student in her own right and devoted her entire life to raising her siblings. They grew up very successful and found good government jobs. She organized their marriages with much fanfare and started living with the eldest and his family. However, her relationship with her sister-in-law soon soured. The younger brother had already begun living separately after marriage. She became a subject of ridicule and torture at the hands of her sister-in-law. Her brother stood by as a mute spectator. Ultimately, she was forced to earn her own living, and was relegated to the basement of the house. She worked in a tailoring house to eke out her living.

Then fate delivered the hardest blow. She met with an accident that almost maimed her. She was unable to work.

She had to depend on her sister-in-law for food, toiletries, medication and other requisites to survive. In six months, the sister-in-law was fed up. She delivered an ultimatum to her to vacate the house and find her own way and place to survive. Her brother did not protest. The other brother never bothered about her.

That is the time when her earlier employer came calling for help and I went myself to fetch her from her house.

At Seneh, she became our most sane and wise resident. All respected her judgement and mature advice. I enjoyed talking to her. Then the worst blow to all of us came when she was diagnosed as suffering from an advanced stage of stomach cancer. We promptly organised a surgery. But it was too late. She succumbed to her illness after three months.

Inadvertently, she said something that I will never forget, and will cherish for the rest of my life. When we were wheeling her into the operation theatre, she was literally howling. I tried to console her and gave her the assurance that nothing will go wrong. What she replied still tastes like elixir to my soul. She said, 'Sir, I am not crying out of fear. It is in the hands of God to decide my future. What you see in my eyes are tears of happiness.

For the first time in my life, I know I am not alone.' I could not stop my tears from rolling down. I did not bother to wipe them.

After her death, one of her nephews appeared, asking us to hand over her death certificate. We refused. He came back with a lawyer. When the young lawyer heard our part of the story, he was exasperated and disgusted and turned against him.

From the last category, I am citing the example of Rinu (name changed). When this stately graduate from an educated family with a long history of psychosis, came to know I was writing the biographies, she herself gave me a seven-page note volunteering her life story written in a neat and clean hand. Unfortunately, I did not find her story compelling enough to be featured in this collection. I do not know how I will explain to her the absence of her story when this book finally sees the light of day.

I wish to end with a translated version of the lyrics of a song that has become the title song of 'Seneh' and is sung as a chorus by all residents, at all functions. I wrote the lyrics, and the lovely tune is the brainchild of Sarala, our visually impaired resident. She has a degree in classical music.

Today we are singing the paeans of our lives
Today we are singing the paeans of our lives
In the womb of Seneh, we attained new lives
We earlier were like withered, fallen flowers,

Painful, merciless tramples kept breaking our hearts,
We experienced in plenty, neglect and spite
Craving for compassion and love, we repeatedly cried,
Fought we did relentlessly, every day, to survive,
Blamed God and his dispensation for our plight.
Seneh ended the excruciating pains of our hearts.
The arrows of abandonment and cruelty broke to pieces.
Today, we are singing the paeans of our lives.
We forgot how to cry, embraced only the smiles
Tied together by Seneh in a common thread,
Sisters we all are, full of contentment and pride.
Today, we are singing the paeans of our lives.

I have a lurking apprehension that the reader may consider this book as an effort to blow my own trumpet. It was never my intention to do that. If in the course of my writing, the 'I' word has appeared repeatedly, it was not by design. It was the truth.